Prepare to
PROFIT

Your Guide to Creating Wealth in
ANY Real Estate Market

Prepare to
PROFIT

Your Guide to Creating Wealth in **ANY** Real Estate Market

Sheri Alford and **Dr. Ahmet Ucmakli**

Tam Tam Press
Murrieta, California

PUBLISHED BY

Tam Tam Press
39252 Winchester Road, Suite 107423
Murrieta, California 92563
PRESS   www.tamtampress.com

Prepare to Profit:
Your Guide to Creating Wealth in ANY Real Estate Market
by Sheri Alford and Dr. Ahmet Ucmakli

———— Publisher's Cataloging-In-Publication Data ————
(Prepared by The Donohue Group, Inc.)

Alford, Sheri.
   Prepare to profit : your guide to creating wealth in any real estate market / Sheri Alford and Ahmet Ucmakli.
      p. ; cm.
   Includes bibliographical references and index.
   ISBN-13: 978-0-9787681-0-2
   ISBN-10: 0-9787681-0-8
1. Real estate investment. 2. Real estate business. I. Ucmakli, Ahmet. II. Title.
HD1382.5 .A44 2007
332.63/24   2006905923

Book and cover design by Peri Poloni-Gabriel
Knockout Design, www.knockoutbooks.com

Edited by Gail M. Kearns
To Press and Beyond, www.topressandbeyond.com

Book Production coordinated by To Press and Beyond

Printed in the United States of America

Table of Contents

✳ ✳ ✳

Chapter 1

Honest Advice

Are you sick and tired of get-rich-quick books and seminars that only make the author rich? So were we. That is precisely why we wrote this book. Anybody can learn how to use a technique or method to invest in real estate, but without the proper team of advisors and backup support, most techniques are bound to fail.

With any investment strategy, you must have a final goal or end point in mind before you can apply any technique. While your goals may actually change along the way, the steps leading up to these goals are crucial and must be properly planned. This is why it is so important to create a team of advisors who will offer you advice on subjects that are not your expertise. While you may be able to become an expert in many fields (over a period of decades!), it is obviously not an efficient way to create real and boundless wealth.

Instead, learn to leverage the expertise of skilled advisors in order to *exponentially* grow your knowledge, and ultimately your wealth, especially in the field of real estate investing. Most of your thoughts and ideas on the subject have already been contemplated and tested. So, unless you are looking to be a pioneer, you don't have to reinvent the wheel in order to create wealth from real estate. Certain investing practices have been in place for decades, and when used properly by a small investor, can yield large rewards. While you are, and should be, the ultimate leader and decision maker of your team, allow respected advisors to guide you closer to your goal.

After gaining a certain amount of experience, you will find that you may differ in opinion with an advisor and ultimately take a different route to something or apply a different technique when investing in a particular property. However, until you gain the necessary experience and wisdom in certain fields go easy on yourself and get surrounded by people in the know who are excited about your impending journey.

Most books on real estate investing today simply focus on specific techniques without giving enough—or any—background information on the team players who should be involved. This would be like a surgeon entering an operation without knowing how an operating-room nurse could help him during the surgery. The surgeon NEEDS assistants or the surgery will not be successful and the patient will likely suffer. In order to avoid any backtrack learning and ultimate suffering, this book will supply you with the needed information and fill in the gaps so that you may start on your journey equipped with the appropriate advisors on your side.

✳ ✳ ✳

Chapter 2

The Benefits of a Team

Real estate investing for the small investor can be a very exciting and profitable venture. It can also cause many gray hairs and heartburn if you do not know what you are doing or if the people that you have hired are not truly knowledgeable leaders in their own field. Having already developed many gray hairs from working in other careers, we wanted to create a book that would help people prevent such difficulties when beginning their journey into real estate investing. We also wanted to describe and explain what really goes on between the steps necessary to creating wealth using real estate. We give you logistics, not theory and attitude like so many other investment books do. So here it is: a book about the truths, the lies, and everything in between that exists in the arena for the small real estate investor. We will teach you which team players are necessary and how to choose them correctly from the beginning.

While this book is not about a certain method or technique to acquire or sell properties, it details the way to go about assembling a team that will help you determine for yourself which methods or techniques best fit your target housing market and your personality. Real estate investing is NOT a one-size-fits-all process as many authors, seminar speakers, and self-proclaimed real estate gurus would like you to believe. Just as the housing market depends on the local economy in your area of interest, so does the method that you use. It is crucial to learn about as many methods of investing in real estate as you can BEFORE you actually plunk down any hard-earned money on a property. Also remember that there are usually multiple ways to make money in real estate. In other words, do not let anybody tell you that he or she knows "the only way to make money" in real estate. This is usually a sign of a professional seminar speaker instead of a tried-and-true real estate investor who could have some useful information.

Many real estate investment seminars taught by authors and self-proclaimed experts espouse techniques of investing that they themselves may have used to make money. That's great, except for one major problem: they used their particular technique years ago, when the market was in some ways very different from what it is now. Remember that the market is an ever-changing scene. So their technique is not a proven method for success in today's market. To top it off, these "gurus" no longer invest in real estate but instead make their living off of selling outdated information through their seminars and books! Invariably, people will go to these courses and seminars and expect to be able to use a specific "script" in order to find a "deal" or a "bargain" and then buy it with "no money down."

Unfortunately, real estate investing is not so easy that you can simply memorize a few lines and *voila,* a bargain or deal is created.

In order to truly be a successful investor, you must become educated and then continue to educate yourself so that you can anticipate opportunities and take advantage of them. Simply memorizing a script from a seminar and repeating it in the field is a total waste of your time and money. Do you think Donald Trump owes his success to a bunch of memorized one-liners?

This is not to say that the techniques taught at seminars cannot make some people some money. The problem is that these methods are not efficient and the seminars can be very costly. Some seminars may be acceptable if you throw away the memorized scripts and just learn the recurring themes that they teach. Better yet, take an educational approach like that taught by Robert Kiyosaki. If you haven't heard of him yet, go get his books (after you read this one, of course). He has a whole series of them. Kiyosaki believes that the only way to real and sustained wealth is through education, not memorization. He encourages people to shift their thinking about money and approach wealth from a new angle. This fresh viewpoint allows you to learn information, absorb it, and then apply it to effective investments such as real estate. A key factor in Kiyosaki's teachings involves surrounding yourself with learned advisors.

Whether you are just beginning your investing or are a seasoned veteran, it is easy to become overwhelmed with all of the great opportunities in real estate. One of your biggest enemies to taking advantage of these opportunities can be your own fear. You can quell these fears by having experienced advisors guiding you and backing your decisions. Success is much more attainable when you don't have to ask *if* something can be done but instead you are concentrating on *how* something can be done.

Utilizing the resources available to you includes getting knowledgeable people to support your actions in theory and finally in execution. Note that not every expert will take the time to help you, but the ones who do are invaluable to your education as well as your ultimate success. These are the people who often remember when they were just starting out and want to see others succeed as well. There's no reason for you to reinvent the wheel, so take advantage of those who came before you.

Once you have a project that involves the purchase of a property or its financing, management, or sale, you will be tempted to take on too much in an effort to control your final destiny and save a few dollars in the process. You may not get very far because you will overwhelm yourself. The beauty of real estate investing is that you don't have to do all the work yourself when you create a team of expert advisors.

In an ideal world, you would wear multiple expert hats, seamlessly perform all tasks related to your business, and save thousands of dollars in the process. Unfortunately, in real estate, you would have to be superhuman and live a very long life in order to become an expert in so many fields. Because running a successful number of investment properties requires knowledge in many facets of business, a single person cannot perform all of the tasks exceptionally well without compromising something important. By trying to do so, a few pennies may be saved, but the lack of quality and efficiency will easily overshadow any pinched pennies.

Don't even try to do the marketing, research, bookkeeping, legal filing, financing, negotiating, advertising, repairs, maintenance, rent collecting, landscaping, bill paying, or contract writing all by yourself. Don't be cheap! Hire someone to get something done right the first time. Free up your time for your most profitable and enjoyable activities.

Given all of the tasks mentioned above, it is difficult to believe that some authors and gurus suggest that success is possible as a part-time real estate investor. If you only have one or two properties, then part time is feasible. However, as the number of your properties grows, so do your responsibilities, making it much more difficult to spend time on other things, like accumulating more properties. While the accumulation of properties is a desirable and achievable goal, you need to ensure that your work and that of your team members is of high quality. Otherwise, you will end up having to do the same task twice, which wastes both time and money.

Build your own expertise on a subject or two while having good functioning knowledge of all others. You can tend to the services that you specialize in, while the other services will require the best representatives that you can find and afford. Don't be afraid to outsource work even from the beginning as you can always take back responsibility at a future date. And remember that just because you are hiring other people to do certain professional tasks doesn't mean you don't need to understand those fields. In order to hire the best experts in each field, you will need to have at least some basic understanding and knowledge in all fields.

Also, be realistic when hiring experts. No one is going to take care of your future and your properties as well as you could if you had all the time and money in the world. With that said, the fact that you have to rely on the work of others means you need to compromise on certain standards that you hold dear. This concept is difficult to grasp sometimes, but it does not suggest that your business will become sub-par or of poor quality. However, it does indicate that you will have to be constantly prioritizing your goals because inevitably, something done by a hired team member will not be completed to your exact standards. The task still may have been done well, but was not exactly what you had in mind. Only you know what your vision holds. Pick your fights carefully and prioritize your goals. If everything has to be done exactly as you wish, then realize that you will have to spend plenty of time communicating your vision as well as spending an inordinate amount of time on every detail of a task. Such actions are not efficient.

While investing in real estate is governed by common sense and routine contracts, there is work involved in creating the wealth. Chosen well, your team of experts can further your efforts exponentially. For example, every region of this country has different factors driving its housing market. You don't always have to know everything about that market as long as you know the people who do.

When you hire or work with experts, don't be intimidated by their knowledge. Instead, use their knowledge to your advantage and their benefit. Don't worry too much about making small mistakes, as it is all part of the process. With a team of expert advisors behind you, your chances of making a mistake will be significantly reduced. With a team, you will also have someone to help analyze the mistakes that do occur so that they can be avoided in the future. Remember, you can be the captain of your team, you just don't need (or even want) to play every position yourself.

Keep in mind that this book will tell you how to find the necessary team members and advisors in order to be a successful real estate investor and make money. However, it is ultimately *you* who has to be willing to find the advisors and use their expertise. Some people will create their team but never really do anything with it. Usually fear is what keeps them from stepping up to the plate. Don't let this be you. We will give you the why, when, and how to invest in real estate, but you have to be willing to DO IT! The team is only as good as its leader...you!

Chapter 3

How to Avoid Getting Crabs

As you embark on your real estate investing career, you will encounter many exciting people who can help you make money. Unfortunately, there are also many people out there who say "you *can't* do that" or "You *used* to be able to make money in real estate but not anymore." We are here to tell you they are the wrong people to listen to.

A friend once told us "not to let these crabs pull us back down into the box." We had no idea what she was talking about. Apparently, when you put several live crabs together in a box, you do not need to use a lid in order to keep them from escaping. Whenever one crab tries to scale the walls of the box to escape, the crabs at the bottom of the box will pull the escapee back down. Without the presence of the other crabs, you would need a lid to stop the progress of the individual renegade crab. Surrounded by other crabs, however, only the rare, perseverant one will clear the clutches of the other cranky crabs and make it to freedom.

Similarly, you can expect friends and family members (yes, people you currently like and respect), as well as strangers (including the media), to attempt to pull you down while you begin your personal ascent to financial freedom. Whether with good intentions (i.e. they don't want to see you hurt) or bad (such as plain old jealously), some people cannot help being negative, life-sucking influences. Unless you are happy in the box with all of the other crabs, you need to find a way to look and live beyond this negativity.

Remember the one rule that not only applies to real estate but to life in general: never say "never" or "always" when it pertains to what is possible. Anything is possible in this crazy world. However, many things may not be probable. The trick is to be able to differentiate between the possible and the probable and to ultimately spend most of your time on the former. Identifying results that are probable simply requires having the appropriate knowledge, which often comes from outside the realm of your own experience. This is why it is so important to surround yourself with the appropriate people who will guide you in the right direction.

Even Donald Trump, one of the most popular real estate investors of our time, does not go it alone. Recently, one of his team players, George H. Ross, a lawyer and Trump advisor, wrote a book entitled *Trump Strategies for Real Estate* that describes his involvement in some of Trump's biggest deals. Ross details how he helps Mr. Trump see the feasibility of certain projects when others believed them to be impossible. Ultimately, Trump and his partners went on to make millions on those deals. The right team of advisors is necessary for ultimate success.

Remember, you will encounter many *crabs* as a real estate investor, regardless of whether you were originally trained as a painter, a doctor, a counselor, or a flight attendant. Throughout this book we will illuminate the truths and the reality of real estate investing, as well as expose many crabs along the way. Here's to your impending freedom!

Chapter 4

Why Real Estate?
Don't Get Us Started!

As you begin putting your team together, you will realize that you need to create a knowledge base of your own regarding the many fields in real estate. Without some basic information on real estate investing and your own personal goals, you could easily be misled by someone of questionable scruples. You must constantly remind yourself of your specific goals or risk getting derailed by a plethora of shamans and snake-oil salesmen.

For those of you not sure why you should invest in real estate, there are four basic reasons. Each potential investment property will have its own unique benefits, but we will go over the four main reasons applicable to every property at one level or another. Whether or not a property excels in one or another of these areas, you will want to consider each of these factors. In an ideal world, your investment property will excel in all four categories. However, in reality, satisfying only one criterion may provide sufficient rewards for your situation. The four criteria are:

1) **Appreciation**

2) **Tax benefits**

3) **Equity buildup or loan repayment (by tenant)**

4) **Cash flow**

Please take the time to truly understand this chapter. It is detail-oriented but short and to the point. It provides you with the foundation to all of your real estate investing decisions and will also provide you with plenty of ammunition against those pesky crabs.

Appreciation

Appreciation is the difference between what the house was originally purchased for and what it can be sold for today. This growth can be measured as a percentage and is then called the *appreciation rate*.

> **Appreciation rate = increase in value/original price**

According to the Office of Federal Housing Enterprise Oversight (OFHEO), in 2005 the national residential-housing appreciation rate was approximately 13 percent, with extremes at both ends of the spectrum.

Appreciation can be astronomical. For example, in 2004, housing prices in Las Vegas skyrocketed at an appreciation rate of 52 percent! This is certainly a year-to-year record for any large metropolitan area and is not the norm (OFHEO).

Appreciation can also be slower in areas such as Utah house and condo prices went up only about 7 percent to 10 percent in the first five *years* of the 2000s. You might think that is not too shabby until you realize that the inflation rate over the same time period was higher, so a property in Utah actually lost value in those years while most of the rest of the country had housing appreciation rates at record levels! However, just because an area has a low appreciation rate does not mean that it is void of any investing value. Remember, a property may excel in one of the other four reasons for investing. Consider all of them when investing. For instance, let's say that a housing market in North Carolina has a yearly appreciation rate of only 3 percent, but rents are very high compared to other similarly priced areas. In this case, you may want to still invest there, forgoing any large appreciation gains in favor of monthly cash flow. We will discuss this later.

While appreciation may be your ultimate goal, how much and how quickly will depend on where and when you buy. Timing in a market plays a large role in appreciation. Real estate investing is a longer-term investment plan, and how long depends on your ultimate goals and needs.

One method of investing is to buy and hold a property for a prolonged period of time. You are basically waiting for the market to create equity for you as time passes. Alternatively, if you are looking for quick cash you may want to sell a property relatively soon after its purchase (assuming that the appreciation rate is sufficiently high). *Flipping*, or selling a property quickly like this for its gains requires experience and expertise.

Both techniques are valid ones and their use is dictated by many factors, including your personal goals and financial situation as well as the condition of the housing market. Remember that any particular housing market can support different successful investing techniques. One size does not fit all.

Tax Advantages

Real estate investing provides a myriad, and we do mean a myriad, of tax benefits. Some are obvious and simple, while others are cloaked in the internal revenue code, which numbers over nine million words! Major deductions will be discussed here while you and your up-to-date accountant can discover some of the lesser known legal loopholes.

First of all, any mortgage interest that you pay for an investment property during the year will be fully tax-deductible. So are any expenses incurred for utilities, repairs, maintenance, homeowner association fees, etc.

Some tax-deductible expenses

- ✔ **Mortgage interest**
- ✔ **Utilities (only those paid by you, not the tenant)**
- ✔ **Repairs**
- ✔ **House maintenance**
- ✔ **Yard maintenance**
- ✔ **Handyman expenses**
- ✔ **Pest control**
- ✔ **Homeowner association fees**
- ✔ **Supplies for the property**
- ✔ **Travel incurred because of the property**
- ✔ **Meals related to investment property activities**

In fact, even though our federal tax code is very complicated, it is very kind to real estate investors in that it encourages citizens to invest in houses, condos, townhomes, and apartments, as well as commercial and industrial properties. We all need places to live and conduct business, and while the government provides for the neediest in society, it cannot and should not provide for everyone. By encouraging private citizens to invest in real estate by offering tax incentives, the government obtains help from the private sector. Investors ultimately provide a bulk of housing for renters and retail space for businesses. As history shows, the private sector is much more efficient and cost-effective at this than the federal, state, or local governments.

Depreciation is another great gift provided by our own federal government and the IRS. While we live in, use, and enjoy our houses, their value generally goes up, providing us with much-loved appreciation. This is especially true of the last ten years or so. However, the government believes that a building only has a limited life span and will eventually need to be replaced, creating a capital expense. Therefore, the government allows owners to *depreciate* a property's value over a certain period of time; 27.5 years for residential buildings and 39 years for most commercial buildings (office, retail, industrial, etc.). So, for every residential investment property, be it a single family residence, condominium, townhome, duplex, three-plex, or four-plex, you can deduct 1/27.5, or roughly 3.63 percent, of the building's value on your taxes every year. In other words, the depreciation from a real estate investment will generally protect an equivalent amount of your regular income from being taxed! When you have multiple properties with higher values, you can see how investing in real estate can significantly lower your tax burden. Remember that this depreciation applies ONLY to the value of the *building* and NOT the land. According to the government, land does not depreciate or lose value over time, and thus it is not depreciable.

In the case of a single family residence, the building usually accounts for approximately 75 percent of your purchase price with the remaining 25 percent attributable to the land. The exact percentages, however, are determined by your local government. So, if you bought a single family residence for $200,000, the portion that is permissible to be depreciated over 27.5 years is equal to 75 percent of $200,000, or $150,000. Oftentimes, to make things easier for quick calculations, we round 27.5 years down to 25 years or 3.63 percent up to 4 percent. This will make your results a little less accurate but easier to determine without a calculator (or even with one). So, returning to our building structure worth $150K, you can deduct roughly 1/25 (or 4 percent) of that, which is $6,000 every year on your taxes. Again, this basically means that $6,000 of money that you earned either from collected rent or from your nine-to-five job will be protected from being taxed by Uncle Sam. Assuming that your highest tax rate for the year is roughly 33 percent, then you just saved $2,000 in taxes based on depreciation alone (33 percent of $6,000 equals $2,000). Not bad for simply owning the property.

Usually, in the case of a condo or a townhome, you will be able to use the *entire* original purchase price as the depreciable amount because the government does not view you as an owner of any land (even though with both types of properties you do have a legal stake in the land underneath). Nonetheless, you can use the entire purchase price to determine your yearly depreciation amount. How sweet it is!

Now there is one caveat with depreciation. If or when you sell a property, the IRS will assume that you and your accountant took the full depreciation allowed to you by law each year that you owned the property, even if you didn't take the deduction! So when you sell an investment, the IRS will levy a tax of 25 percent on those deductions that it assumes you took, in what is called a *recapture tax*. They are basically "recapturing" some of what they offered to you in the first place. What the IRS giveth, the IRS taketh away. But wait. In the case of our $200,000 home earlier, with the $150K of usable depreciation we applied over roughly 25 years, we took a $6,000 depreciation every year. The IRS will recapture 25 percent of this yearly deduction taken; in this case it is 25 percent of $6,000, or $1,500. Summing it up, the government allowed us to save $2,000 every year after taxes because of depreciation alone, while only taking back $1,500 a year at sale time. Basically, we still net $500 for every year that we owned this one property. And this applies ONLY if you sell the property and pocket the capital gain. In addition, there are legal ways of deferring tax payments such as these, through a 1031 exchange, which will be discussed in detail later.

Depreciation also applies to certain items in a building besides the building itself. Anything that is not permanently attached to an investment property but is integral to the function and utility of the house is considered a *chattel*. These things are essentially movable property. Chattels include items such as large kitchen appliances, window coverings, carpeting, cabinetry, ceiling fans, etc. Again, the IRS allows a real estate investor to depreciate these items over a period of time, depending on the particular item. Usually they are depreciated over five years.

You can roughly estimate chattels to be about 5 percent to 6 percent of the purchase price of the property; however, it is strongly recommended that you hire a professional chattels appraiser, as he or she should be more up to date on IRS instructions. A professional appraisal of this kind will also provide more legitimacy to your accounting numbers and methods, which can come in handy if you ever get audited by the IRS. The chattels appraiser is an important team player who will be discussed later in this book.

So for our $200K sample house, the estimated value of the chattels would be approximately 6 percent of $200,000, which equals $12,000. Spreading this $12K over 5 years, your annual deduction would be about $2,400. Again, assuming a tax rate of 33 percent, this would amount to a savings of $800 per year. The first year's tax benefits from this appraisal would make the appraiser's fee well worth it. Isn't the government just so generous? Okay, you don't really have to answer that question.

In addition to depreciation and the other numerous deductions, the IRS uses tax credits to encourage investors to offer certain kinds of specialty housing to the public. A tax credit is considerably better than a deduction. With a credit, every dollar you spend on a qualified property will get you a dollar decrease in your ultimate tax liability. With a deduction, your ultimate tax savings depends on your final tax rate for the year. So with our current tax rates, the most one can save on one dollar of deductions is thirty-five cents. We'll take a tax credit over a tax deduction any day.

As mentioned earlier, while federal, state, and local governments do provide some housing for our most impoverished citizens, they still need the assistance of the private sector. As a result, tax credits are available to those investors willing to provide low-income housing. Tax credits are also available to investors who buy properties that are on the National Register of Historic Places as well as houses that were simply built before 1936. Our nation's tax laws encourage this type of entrepreneurship in order to help maintain and restore these historical places and the heritage that comes with them, all the while providing a fabulous place for some of our citizens to live in.

A crucial step in attaining the most tax benefits from your real estate investments will come when you work with an excellent certified public accountant (CPA). He or she must know the tax code as it relates to real estate investing, have ample resources, and stay abreast of the multitude of changes occurring to the tax code nearly every year. All tax accountants are not the same. Don't just open up the yellow pages and pick the one with the best ad. Instead, thoroughly research, interview, and choose accountants who specialize in working with small real estate investors. Your CPA should know much more than you do.

A friend who owned several investment properties told us that her tax accountant advised her against taking the tax deductions offered to real estate investors because "it was too much of a hassle." As a result, she ended up with absolutely *no* tax benefits from her real estate investments. It was later revealed to us that the accountant was actually her father, who owned no investment properties of his own. She may have saved some money in accountant fees, but ultimately lost thousands upon thousands of dollars in legal deductions because she refused to pay an expert for his or her time. Also remember that when she sells her properties in the future, the government will levy the recapture tax on her profits even though she did not take the deductions available to her at the time she owned the properties. This was a costly mistake on her part.

When you start to specialize in your investing, you will need up-to-date and aggressive team members and expert advisors. In our friend's case, her father did not know about or was not comfortable with tax accounting for the small real estate investor even though he was a CPA. Obviously not the right team member. When the government offers a legal deduction to you, don't hesitate to take it.

Another option for tax accounting, franchised tax service companies for the masses, are fine for just that—the masses. As proof, one of the largest and most successful tax service franchises in the U.S., a household name, does not even require their employees to take any continuing education classes in their field of tax preparation! In fact, just before tax season every year, this conglomerate places newspaper ads throughout the country looking to fill its seasonal tax jobs. This is certainly not a company you would want to entrust with your hard-earned money and especially with your specialized tax situation. Usually there is a reason that a service is inexpensive. As an astute real estate investor, you must consider tax consequences at every stage of the process, not only during a seasonal tax time.

Equity Buildup or Loan Repayment

When you lease your house to well-screened tenants, they agree to pay you a monthly rent for an agreed-upon time period. The money that you collect should go towards paying the property's expenses. Let's assume that your mortgage payment on an investment property is $1000 per month for thirty years and that you collect $1000 per month in rent from your tenants. Congratulations! You have received enough money to pay the mortgage each month. Assuming your loan payment consists of principal and interest (P&I), some of the payment each month goes towards *decreasing* the principal amount that you borrowed. Therefore, for every month of every year that your tenants pay rent, they are paying down your mortgage. How much they pay off depends on the exact terms of your loan and how much of each monthly payment is actually principal. This information can easily be found in an amortization table.

Assuming a best-case scenario of great tenants who pay the rent every month and stay for the duration of the mortgage (thirty years in this case), their rent payments will completely pay off your loan. As a result, you will own the house free and clear at the end of thirty years. Also assuming that the property is in excellent shape and was bought in a very desirable area with a healthy local economy, you should have a significant amount of equity in just this one property, all of which can be liquified with a sale.

This concept remains quite lucrative, even when you consider the other costs of an investment property. Besides principal (P) and interest (I), you will have to pay property taxes (T) and insurance (I). Often, these are combined in the acronym PITI. In addition, you will also have to cover maintenance, utilities, homeowner association fees, periods of vacancy, etc. Depending on the amount of rent you are able to secure each month, these additional costs may or may not exceed your monthly rental income. If the monthly rent is not sufficient to cover these items, then you will be paying for them yourself out of your pocket, resulting in a negative cash flow situation. The ultimate goal is to have at least a major portion of your expenses, if not all, covered by the rent.

Cash Flow

In an ideal investing world, not only will the tenant's monthly rental payments cover your expenses, they will exceed them. This would mean that you are receiving extra money every month, i.e. positive cash flow, after all expenses are paid. If your monthly expenses exceed the rent payments coming in from tenants, then you have negative cash flow. Every investor wants positive cash flow on his or her investments, but look carefully to determine the difference between before-tax and after-tax cash flow. Whereas before-tax cash flow may be negative or a few dollars in hand, the after-tax cash flow is money saved from going towards taxes and is almost always significantly larger than the before-tax cash flow.

Let's look at our example of a $200,000 house (which, by the way, was chosen because it is roughly the median price of a home in the United States as of the writing of this book). If we have a $1,000 per month mortgage payment on this house, plus $500 per month of other expenses (utilities, vacancy, management fees, etc.), but only receive $1,000 per month in rent, then our before-tax cash flow is a negative $500 per month, or a negative $6000 per year. At first glance these numbers look fruitless in your effort to build wealth, but never fear—tax deductions are here!

As mentioned before, most, if not all, of the $500 property expenses are tax-deductible. On a $200,000 loan, the deductible interest portion of the P&I is roughly $800 per month (this number will vary based on loan terms; therefore, look at an amortization table for exact numbers). And finally, don't forget the yearly deduction we calculated earlier for depreciation of approximately $500 per month, or $6,000 per year.

Various deductible expenses/mo	$500
Deductible interest payments/mo	$800
Deductible building depreciation/mo	$500
Total deductions	($1,800/month)
X 12 months equals	($21,600/year)

Multiplied by twelve months, we have $21,600 of yearly total deductions. The parenthesis indicates that this is considered a negative number, or a loss, as far as the IRS is concerned. Since we collected $1,000 per month rent or $12K for the year, on paper we lost $9,600 for the year. Wait, where did that number come from?

Yearly "loss" (from above)	($ 21,600)
Yearly rental income	$ 12,000
Total yearly gain or loss	($ 9,600)

Again, because this number is negative, it indicates a loss, at least on paper. Therefore, the IRS allows you take an equivalent tax deduction for this particular property. In other words, you will keep $9,600 of hard-earned income from being taxed at all. So, assuming a high tax rate of roughly 33 percent, your tax bill will be 33 percent of $9,600 or $3,168 less because of this one property. Dividing $3,168 by twelve months gets you $264 per month of after-tax savings. Another way of saying this is that each month, you will pay $264 less in taxes. Imagine if you had four similar properties. You would save roughly $1,000 dollars in taxes per month or $12,000 per year. Summarizing this situation, we went from an actual loss of $500 per month before taxes to a positive cash flow of $264 per month. Not too shabby! However, if you did not have the understanding of before- and after-tax cash flows, then you probably would never consider this property as an investment. Knowledge is king. Of course, remember that your actual after-tax savings will depend upon your own personal tax rate.

Again, as you can see, what appears at first glance to be a severe monthly negative cash flow before taxes will often become positive cash flow after taxes. There are actually many computer software programs in the marketplace that, with a few basic numbers provided by you for a particular property, can show the pre- and post-tax cash flows. Dolf de Roos, international real estate investor and author, has created a software program called Real Estate Assessment Program or REAP©, which is very effective and very easy to use. Go to www.dolfderoos.com for more information.

So now you know the four simple but compelling reasons for buying real estate as an investment. The reasons can work together or compensate for one another. Use professional help to evaluate each factor before you make an investment. You may not see the strength or weakness of an investment initially, but an expert will because he or she is trained to view the investment that way. The more you surround yourself with knowledgeable advisors, the more you will be able to identify good investment opportunities.

Remember that real estate investing is NOT about luck or being in the right place at the right time. It is about being prepared to act when an opportunity is presented or created. Successful real estate investing is not a random occurrence. As you gain more experience, you will find that you see opportunities where others do not.

Stocks versus Real Estate

To further illustrate the benefits of real estate investing, let's compare real property to stocks as investments vehicles. There are many types of investment mediums besides real estate that are available to the general public today, including stocks, bonds, mutual funds, commodities, gold, silver, and so on. In fact, today, roughly 50 percent of the public in the United States owns stocks, whereas fifty years ago, less than 10 percent owned any paper assets. We believe that real estate investing is undergoing a similar change, in that more and more people are becoming involved in buying properties for their investment potential. However, real estate better maintains its many benefits when compared to stocks.

The main advantage of real estate over stocks is one of leverage. When acquiring real estate, the banks legally allow you to use their money to fund most, if not all, of your purchase. Usually, lenders like to see that you are sharing the risk by pitching in some of your own money, in the form of a down payment. For example, the bank may require that you come up with a 10 percent down payment to purchase a $200,000 home. Thus, the borrower must come up with $20K for the down payment at closing in order to borrow $180,000 from the bank.

Now it would be very difficult, if not impossible, for you to borrow $180,000 from a bank in order to purchase $200K of stocks, bonds, mutual funds, or other kinds of paper assets. It is just not ordinarily done. Purchases of these kinds of assets are done dollar for dollar. In other words, with $20,000, you can obtain only $20,000 in stocks. While with that same $20,000, you can reasonably purchase $200,000 worth of real estate.

This leveragability allows the real estate investor to gain appreciation on the entire $200,000 investment instead of appreciation on merely the $20K worth of stocks that the shareholder has. By viewing real estate in this manner, it becomes apparent that the appreciation rate itself is not the whole picture when comparing stocks to real estate. The principal amount which can appreciate in value is significantly larger with real estate since you've leveraged yourself into a greater ownership position.

> **Assume that your initial investment in each example below is $20, 000:**
>
> **10 percent appreciation on $20K stocks=$ 2,000, but**
>
> **10 percent appreciation on $200K of real estate = $20,000!**

Using the above example, if stocks and real estate both appreciate by 10 percent in one year, you can see that with real estate you will have doubled your initial investment. In other words, the true appreciation rate on your initial investment of $20,000 would be 100 percent instead of 10 percent! Meanwhile, with the stocks, a 10 percent appreciation rate really means ONLY 10 percent.

Another advantage that real estate has over stocks is in the treatment of capital gains. When an investor makes a profit from the sale of stocks or real estate, there is a capital gains tax paid to the federal government (and most state governments). With stocks, unless you have significant *losses* from other investments, it is difficult to legally bring down the amount of tax you will have to pay on that gain. With real estate, as discussed in detail earlier, the tax shelter is practically built in, with the inclusion of many deductions. In addition, when you sell a real estate investment, the costs that go into preparing, repairing, and selling the property are deductible, which ultimately helps to bring down the amount of capital gains tax that you will have to pay. This advantage can save the real estate investor thousands of dollars when the time comes to pay tax on capital gains.

Naysayers will point out that real estate investing requires more time, energy, and money, whereas with stocks you simply hire an advisor to make decisions for you. Be careful about casually turning over control of your wealth to someone else, as no one will care about your money as much as you do. By listening to only a single broker or financial planner, you limit your options to whatever he or she may know about. Any time you entrust someone else with your financial health, we propose that you do so with an advisory team of experts. If you are putting together a team, why not do it in the exciting world of real estate, with all of its benefits? The rewards will be well worth your effort.

Chapter 5

The Purchase Team

Vital team members and advisors for the purchase of an investment property include:

1) **Real estate agent or Realtor®**

2) **Loan officer or mortgage broker**

3) **Appraiser**

4) **Escrow/title company**

5) **Real estate attorney**

6) **Home inspector**

7) **Insurance agent**

8) **Chattels appraiser**

9) **Entity expert for corporations and asset protection**

10) **Spouse or significant other (this team member is actually important for every stage in your investing, as well as your life!)**

Real Estate Agent or Realtor®

The real estate agent is one of the most important team members that you can have during the purchase, management, and selling of your property. In other words, a good one is priceless. A *Realtor®* is a real estate licensee who is a member of the National Association of Realtors®. As such, he or she has signed a written agreement to provide a high level of customer service and professional standards. Realtors® also have access to exceptional educational resources and opportunities. We recommend looking for the Realtor® logo in order to increase your chance of finding someone who is committed to helping you.

Realtors® have astounding informational resources available to them, and it is their job to impart this knowledge to you, the client. They may be your best resource for finding information on a city, a certain block, or a particular house when beginning your search for a property. Whereas you may be unfamiliar with a particular area, an agent may have done a transaction there recently and knows everything from current property values to taxes to homeowner association issues. Available only to agents in its most detailed form, the Multiple Listing Service (MLS) catalogs properties for sale and pertinent information in one tidy place. Professional agents usually also have access to elaborate networks of professionals and other potential team members or advisors that would take years for you to create on your own. There is no need to reinvent the wheel.

Having open lines of communication is essential with this team member. In this industry, time is money. Agents are not paid unless a transaction is completed, so you need one who will persevere until the last "i" is dotted and the last "t" is crossed. Respect their time by only using their services for appropriate and necessary tasks. Don't ask them to clean up an unwanted situation that you created in the first place. Be honest when you talk with an agent. Are you really ready to buy or sell? Are you just looking for information? Interview several before you actually make use of their services. When you have made a choice, use that agent exclusively in order to build rapport, loyalty, and trust. Using an agent for information only, then taking your business elsewhere, can end up hurting you in the long run by burning bridges and creating a negative reputation for yourself in the community. The right agent will listen to what your goals and needs are, find the desired property, and ultimately guide you in a transaction. But do remember that ALL of the ultimate decisions and responsibilities to buy or sell a property are yours and yours alone. As a coveted team member, the agent is there to properly advise and guide you through a real estate transaction.

Good agents spend a lot of time and money to help you purchase a property. They spend hard-earned money on gas, car, phone, advertising, and other services in order to better help you and their other clients. Having said this, pay them accordingly. If you ask for a discount, you will receive a discounted effort, as this is simply human nature. Don't be cheap! It's not worth it in the long run.

How to Choose a Real Estate Agent

Ask around. Talk to people who are doing what you want to be doing, i.e. buying real estate as an investment. Interview plenty of agents but respect their time. Remember that an interview does not have to be anything formal. A simple phone conversation in which you ask some important questions may suffice. However, if you wish, you can ask an agent for a more formal presentation. Ultimately, you will be spending a good deal of time with your agent so you will need a good connection.

The agent you choose must have access to resources besides the MLS, resources such as local market data, publications, websites, association memberships, and client and professional networks, to name just a few. Good agents actively seek out information in order to stay abreast of changes in the real estate field instead of waiting for the information to come to them. By the time it falls in their laps, the news will be old and less useful. Find out how a potential agent stays on top of market changes. An agent should know significantly more regarding his or her job than you or the average citizen who reads the newspaper. Multiple sources for information are essential.

Experience with investors is also a must-have! This way your agent will understand your investment needs better, as criteria to buy a house to *live in* can be very different. For instance, a buyer looking for a home to occupy may have feng shui as a major criterion when buying, but a seasoned investor will not worry about such a subjective issue (you'd be amazed by what some investors think is important). Your agent should be aware of such differences. And if the agent has experience with investors, he or she will already have connections to other people who may assist you, such as loan officers, renters, buyers, etc.

Find out if potential agents do any real estate investing themselves. If someone is working in this business, with all of the opportunities around them, and still does not own anything, you gotta wonder why.

Finally, a positive attitude is important. You don't want to start out with someone who says "that can't be done." Just because something hasn't already been done doesn't mean it can't be done. Experience will affect this too. A good agent will suggest ideas that you haven't yet considered.

Loan Officer or Mortgage Broker

Leverage, sometimes referred to as *other people's money* or OPM, is a key ingredient to successful investing. Not many beginning investors will have hundreds of thousands of dollars in their bank accounts in order to purchase property. The loan officer or mortgage broker is the person who assists you in this search for money and originates (i.e. processes) your loan. He or she should be in constant communication with the lender (also called "the investor") who is providing the money for your purchase.

A good loan officer will help match the appropriate loan product with your needs, as there is a cornucopia of loan products available to the investor today. You must communicate to the loan officer whether you are most interested in the smallest down payment or lowest monthly payment versus any other special needs. Armed with your personal wish list, the loan officer can shop your loan by researching the types of loans available at any given time. Loan officers will also discuss with you the costs of borrowing money, including, but not limited to, their own fees. Some costs and fees specific to a loan will vary, but a broker's fee should be a predictable amount. So have loan officers reveal standard fees even before they run your credit—you don't want any surprises. Ultimately, stick with a good loan officer for at least several loans because the more business you do with that person, the more room you will have to negotiate fees. Not to mention that he or she will know more about what you are looking for.

If you own only one home (i.e. your own) and have good credit, as well as a respectable income, getting a decent loan should be fairly easy. However, the more properties you have, the more obstacles you will encounter. At some point, you will have to provide extensive documentation with regards to where your money comes from and where it goes to. The more complicated your financial file, the more they will want to know. So be prepared to provide copies of your last two years of tax returns, two months of pay stubs, and two months of bank statements. Having these documents ready for the loan officer will save time and make the loan process more efficient.

The mortgage industry expects a borrower to jump through a series of hoops before it will lend you the money necessary to fund your purchase. This can be a very frustrating process for investors, as you really have no recourse but to play their game. Jump through their hoops as best as you can without getting angry or injured. Then, when you come out a winner on the other side of the hoops, give yourself a pat on the back.

Remember that the underwriters who scrutinize your loan application materials are hired by the lenders and have, as an ultimate objective, to safeguard the lender's money. The lender will only fund your deal if they believe that you and the property in question are a reasonable risk with their money. In other words, is it likely that you will pay them back as agreed to in the contract? The underwriters will ultimately make this decision and act accordingly. Don't be discouraged, though, when the underwriter keeps throwing you and your loan officer curve balls. Even if you have excellent credit scores and financial statements, convincing the underwriters of your worthiness can sometimes be a daunting task. This is when good loan officers can earn their fees. If a loan officer has a good relationship with an underwriter, the officer can influence the underwriter in a positive manner if there is a question or an unusual situation arises. Without this close rapport, your fate will be completely left up to a series of computations made by the underwriter.

The loan process can get even more complicated when you own more than a certain number of homes. This is due to requirements set forth by the Federal National Mortgage Association, or Fannie Mae for short. Fannie Mae was initially created in 1938 as an agency of the federal government. However, in 1968 it was rechartered by Congress as a private corporation. In the early twentieth century, as a result of increased demand for mortgages, banks were doling out all of the funds available to them and were essentially running out of money. To remedy the situation, Fannie Mae was formed in order to buy these mortgages from the banks at a discounted rate, allowing the banks to continue their lending practices with replenished coffers. In fact, the creation of Fannie Mae helped to spur the U.S. economy out of the Great Depression.

Today, Fannie Mae is the largest purchaser of mortgages on the secondary market and has become a multi-billion-dollar corporation. It is in this secondary market that Fannie Mae buys mortgages (also called notes) from other lenders. As a result of this system, most lenders today want to *conform* to the rules and regulations created by Fannie Mae so that they too can sell their notes to Fannie Mae after the loan is closed. This kind of loan is called a *conforming loan* and is very common. Generally, conforming loans will have better terms and rates for the borrower and are easier to obtain. This is because the lender knows that it will be able to sell your loan to Fannie Mae or other such institutions.

Fannie Mae's regulations determine the ease with which you can acquire certain types of loans. For instance, as mentioned above, if you own ten properties or more (with corresponding mortgages), you may not qualify for a conforming loan. Thus, getting financing at this level may become problematic instead of becoming easier, as one might think. But not to worry: this circumstance is problematic, but not impossible. Situations like this will require a knowledgeable and tenacious loan officer, someone who will go the extra mile for you and find an acceptable loan product.

Another entity involved in the world of real estate financing is the Federal Home Loan Mortgage Corporation or Freddie Mac. In 1970, the U.S. Government formed this entity for the purpose of creating an even larger secondary market for residential mortgages. Combined, Fannie Mae and Freddie Mac have become the largest holders of mortgages in the country and play vital roles in the stability of the housing market. So as you can see, in general, you don't have a lot of control over the basic terms of traditional financing as they are dictated by the standards of the secondary market. Even Donald Trump has to abide by the same rules when using conventional funding.

Types of Loans

There are ways to legally get around the requirements of these conforming loans, but it will cost you a premium. *Hard money lenders* are private investors who have plenty of money that they are willing to loan you for the purchase of a property. The interest rates on these types of loans are much higher than traditional bank loans and come with shorter and more stringent terms. If, however, you are in a bind, or find a great deal when you are short of cash, a hard money lender may play a temporary role in the game of investing. You should consider all of your options before working with a hard money lender.

Especially over the past few years, the number of conventional loan products available to home buyers and investors has increased dramatically. Just five years ago, the most common and easiest loan to get in the U.S. was the thirty-year fixed loan. This means that the interest rate is fixed for thirty years (i.e. throughout the term of the loan), and monthly payments include principal and interest.

As recently as 2004, if you asked a lender about *interest-only* loans for residential properties, you would have received a quizzical response. Nowadays, interest-only loans are exceedingly common-place in certain high-priced regions of the country. These can be very helpful with cash flow in certain circumstances. In fact, many other countries, such as the United Kingdom, Australia, and New Zealand, have been using interest-only loans in their residential markets for quite some time while in the United States they have been reserved for commercial properties until only recently.

Lenders know that the average American stays in his or her house for only approximately five to ten years before moving up to a bigger or better property. In response, lenders have tailored more loans to fit this timeframe. Lately, using an *adjustable rate mortgage* or an ARM has become exceedingly popular in residential markets. This array of loan products include 1/1, 3/1, 5/1, 7/1, and 10/1 ARMs. The first number indicates the number of years that the interest rate will be fixed, while the second number indicates how often, in years, the interest rate will change after the initial fixed period. What's the advantage? Because banks realize that you are taking a risk by only fixing the rate for a small period of time, they reward you with a lower initial interest rate, called a *teaser*. Rewards have their risks, of course. For instance, if after the fixed period of time the rates skyrocket, your monthly payments will also increase. However, if you only plan to hold on to an investment property for a few short years, the ARMs' low rates can be very useful. Longer-term investments can also benefit from ARMs as long as you can refinance periodically into better loan products when rates go too high. Even though the original use of the term "mortgage" is derived from French and Latin meaning "an agreement until death," it no longer has to last that long.

Another controversial but potentially beneficial loan product for investors is the interest-only loan. Monthly payments are simply payments of interest that you owe for the privilege of borrowing the money. At the end of a designated time period, the principal is due in full. This is called a *balloon payment*, since it is considerably larger than what you have been paying each month. Of course, these interest payments are less than paying both interest and a portion of principal. Because of its lower monthly payments, the interest-only loan can also help create a positive cash flow situation for a desirable property.

Some people believe that interest-only loans are dangerous and consider them to be exotic. The only thing exotic about them may be that they were used in places like New Zealand and Australia well before they became popular in the U.S. Their lower monthly payments can actually help you buy a larger, more expensive property or simply help you to cash flow. However, if you choose an interest-only loan, then you must also be responsible enough to budget your finances in order to pay the balloon payment at the end of the term by either selling the property or refinancing the loan. You must also be relatively certain that your market will continue to appreciate (even if at a very low rate). Otherwise, you can end up being *upside-down*, meaning that you owe more money on the loan than the house is worth. It's also important that you have enough money available should the interest rates rise during the *variable* portion of your loan.

Since the payments of an interest-only loan consist simply of interest, none of your payments will actually reduce the principal amount that you owe. So of course this means that the principal owed on an interest-only loan will not be reduced at all over the years of ownership unless you make additional payments. On our $200K sample home with a 6 percent interest-only loan, yearly payments would be 6 percent of $200K or $12,000 a year. Divided by twelve months we have a mortgage of $1,000 per month. Using a P&I loan with the same amount and interest rate, the monthly payment would be approximately $1,200 or $200 per month more than the interest-only variety. If you are planning to keep the property for a short period of time and you can safely predict at least a 2 to 3 percent yearly appreciation rate on the house, then an interest-only loan may be ideal for improving your cash flow position. In fact, much of commercial real estate is purchased with interest-only financing.

These types of loans are definitely not for the irresponsible who will merely waste the saved money that goes into their pockets. Use interest-only loans and ARMs only when you are fairly confident that the house can be resold later for more than the original purchase price and that you have the fiscal responsibility that it requires.

To further complicate your financing choices, there are hybrid loans that take aspects of different loans and combine them into one. For instance, there are interest-only ARMs available to investors, as well as loans that give you the option to change the kind of loan payment plan you have every month! These are called *pay-option ARMs*.

Study the market and make your loan choice carefully. Hopefully, in this section, we were able to impress upon you the importance of staying current in the ever-changing world of mortgage financing. And if financing is not your forte, then utilize the expertise of your loan officer. First, though, make sure that you understand and speak the loan officer's language.

All of this information is critical for two reasons. First of all, you will need these tools as an arsenal for various investing strategies. Second, you need to know what a good loan officer should be exposing you to. Again, the ultimate choice of loan is yours, but a good loan officer can help coach you in the right direction. Even when you have experience with loans, the experts can introduce you to new and exciting loan products that may be of benefit to your situation.

Jumping through Hoops

As mentioned earlier, you will find that many lenders will ask you to jump through a varying number of hoops before lending you money for a property. Sometimes, once you think that you have fulfilled all of their requests and that there could be no more conditions or requirements, a new hoop is presented and this time it comes with a ring of fire surrounding it! Try not to take these demands personally. However, it is surely a test of wills and requires a good deal of patience. If you truly want the property, you will put on a good pair of cross-training shoes and a fire-resistant jumpsuit and then steadfastly jump through each and every hoop, ending the obstacle course with only minor scratches.

This is not to say that you won't get frustrated, as there will be times that you question the value of continuing. Remember that the lender does this with most people (probably even with Donald Trump to a certain extent) and is only protecting the lenders' money by weeding out people who do not have the stomach to deal with potentially stressful situations like investing in real estate.

Spending the Night with Our Loan Officer

No, we're not encouraging you to use dubious tactics to get the best loan! Instead, we want you to learn from our experience, so allow us to share a story. From it, you will hopefully glean the difference that a great loan officer can make and how to spot one. Here's our true story.

After a few transactions with the same mortgage broker, we believed that we had established a good rapport and brought him more business of our own as well as referring fellow investors. We discovered our referrals were keeping him very busy. Unfortunately, as a result, our file was passed onto a lower-ranking processor in the office when the new, "bigger" clients arrived (the same ones that we referred to him). No longer were our calls returned, nor were our deadlines being met. Even though we provided all of the requested information for two pending purchases, our new contact person felt no tie to us. She had no problem missing work and eventually quit without notice. In fact, not only did *she* disappear, but she did so with some of our files!

Meanwhile, our closing dates, set by the builders, came and went, but no loans were secured for us. We were informed that because this took place during the December holidays, no one in the office would be able to help us to secure a loan until after the New Year. Unfortunately, this would be too late for the sellers, as they were already harassing us to close on the two properties. By going beyond the designated closing date, we ran the risk of the builder cancelling our contracts and legally keeping our combined earnest deposits of ten thousand dollars.

Frantically calling every loan officer we'd ever spoken to or worked with, we desperately searched for someone to help us get loans immediately. We asked agents, other loan officers, anyone who might know someone who could help. Even hard money lenders were difficult to reach at this time of the year. Finally, we did locate a loan officer who, after hearing the basics of our situation, thought that he could save our properties if we could provide him with a complete file. So we went back to our original broker to obtain our files.

Amazingly, the original mortgage broker acted insulted when we requested our files in order to try this new broker. Their definition of loyalty obviously differed from ours. We guess they expected us to stay loyal to the end even though their actions (or inactions in this case) would have resulted in huge losses for us. Luckily, though, between what they provided and the extensive copies of documents that we kept at home, we met the new loan officer fully armed with documentation.

After nearly five hours of discussing and reviewing our file—on New Year's Eve, no less—our new friend expressed confidence in being able to make this happen. Because our portfolio was strong and our credit was good, he thought that everything would make sense to the in-house underwriter, with whom he had developed a good relationship. There was one catch, though. Given the time constraints, he could only save one property, and since condominiums require additional loan paperwork, we let that one go to save the single family home that had even more equity than the condo. The lost earnest deposit from the condominium would have to be claimed as a capital loss in next year's tax returns. The potential down payment that we had saved up for the condominium was then applied to the down payment of the single family home, which made obtaining its loan that much easier.

Believe it or not, come January 2, at 9:00 A.M., our new loan officer had us approved by the underwriter and obtained loan documents for us to sign. All of this in less than twenty-four hours! Normally, a very fast closing is considered two weeks, with a fairly standard one being thirty days. This wasn't a normal situation, but our loan officer stepped up to the plate and met the challenge. He hit a pinch-hit homerun for us. Ultimately, by having our entire file ready and finding the right team member, we were able to save the house and all of its equity, approximately $100,000.

This is the type of loan officer who deserves your business and your loyalty. Someone like this who is willing to go that extra mile not only receives the commission from that loan, but also from all of your future business. In addition, we were happy to have found someone with integrity. However, don't expect that your first try will necessarily yield you this type of quality; it may take scouting through a few loan officers, but hopefully you will not have to experience a situation like the one we did.

You can find loan officers through any number of resources such as your banking institution; your Realtor®; a family or friend's recommendation; TV, print, or radio advertising; etc. Mortgage brokers and loan officers are professionals hungry for business, and you'll see plenty of promises out there for the "lowest rates," "no fees," and "fast" closings. No one can truly tell you specific numbers without some of your financial information. So, be wary of unsubstantiated promises and claims. Don't allow your credit to be run without some basic information on the broker or on how they make their money. The best loan officer can save you valuable time and money—the worst can waste both.

How to Find a Good Loan Officer

A referral speaks volumes if it comes from someone that you respect. Realtors® with investor experience will have worked with loan officers who also have experience with other investors. Opinions formed from these experiences can be invaluable. Don't just get a name, though. Find out why this person is so highly regarded. Was it that the loan officer paid the agent a referral fee, or was it that the loan officer really hustled to close the deal on time?

Experience with investors is mandatory for a loan officer, as loans for homeowners can be very different than those for investors. Like a good real estate agent, a good loan officer should know the latest changes in the industry. He or she should also understand different loan products, along with their advantages and disadvantages. Don't be the guinea pig for a loan officer who has no connections or experience. Your money is too important. Since you are the one making the final decisions, insist on viewing loan options instead of simply accepting "the loan that we use for all our investors."

Getting a loan is not always going to be a wild, down-to-the wire situation like the one we described earlier. Nonetheless, an excellent loan officer should be able to anticipate and preempt most major problems. A loan officer's commitment should not be based on the amount of the loan or his or her commission. Ideally, work with a loan officer who also has a support team, as simple but important tasks like returning phone calls are much easier to do if he or she has help. A good assistant can free up a loan officer's time to be productive on closings while still keeping you informed. Communication from the loan officer is absolutely essential because without it you won't be able to remedy a problem that the underwriter might raise. So find out exactly who will be handling your file—don't be passed on to a stranger once you are locked in.

While communication is essential from your loan officer, you should make the effort to understand the nuances of the loans that he or she recommends. Respect your loan officer's time and efforts, and be realistic with your expectations as there are many loan guidelines and restrictions that loan officers are legally obligated to follow. Loan officers have no power to change those guidelines. When you are asked for documentation, get it to them promptly, or better yet, have basic documentation copied and ready to go at your first meeting. The loan officer will be very pleased and impressed. Ultimately, your loan officer will be a better team player if you pass him or her the ball.

Appraiser

Appraisers have the tough job of assigning a home's value. They are independent, yet they are influenced by various groups of people. Sellers hope for the highest amount from the appraiser so that they can receive the highest price at the sale. In general, the lender looks for a low figure from an appraisal so that they don't have to lend as much money, thus reducing their risk. And finally, buyers usually want an appraisal higher than the sales price to know they got a deal—but they also wouldn't mind it being lower so they can get the seller to drop the price. It all depends on the situation. With all of these different opinions, appraisers must somehow stay impartial when judging the value of a property. To help them walk the straight and narrow, they use three objective approaches in order to make the appraisal.

1) **The comparative approach**

2) **The replacement approach**

3) **The income approach**

The Comparative Approach

Using *comparable sales,* or *comps,* the appraiser will contrast the cost of other like properties within a certain distance of the subject property. Comparative factors include, but are not limited to, price per square foot, lot size, quality of building materials, age of the property, upgraded features, etc. The comparative approach is used most often for residential real estate.

The Replacement Approach

This method views the value of the property from the standpoint of actually having to replace it. So if something physically happened to the property, i.e. if it is destroyed by fire, flood, earthquake, etc., how much would it cost to rebuild using similar materials? This method is considered the most accurate, but most often gives the lowest appraised value. Thus, insurers prefer this method when appraising a property's value so that their payout during a claim is acceptable but relatively low.

The Income Approach

In this final method, the appraiser bases the value on the market income (i.e. monthly rent) that can be expected from a particular property. By taking the yearly income previously received from a property and dividing it by the cost of the property, they create a ratio called the *capitalization rate* or *cap rate*. Commercial real estate professionals focus greatly on this number since these properties are strictly investment vehicles.

As you can see, appraisers can often make or break a deal, depending on what method is used and who holds their loyalty. While there is often not much you can do to change a given appraisal, you have the right to ask questions and bring up certain factors that the appraiser may overlook or may even not be aware of, such as upgrades in the subject property and recent sales in your neighborhood that did not go through the MLS. In booming areas, appraisers are often in short supply, so those that are available can be stretched thin and, like any of us in an overworked situation, can accidentally overlook or miss important factors.

The appraisal will be integral during the early part of the purchase. By assigning a third party to determine the value of a property, it allows all parties involved to determine whether an agreement or contract on a property will continue to the next step or if it will have to be renegotiated. Often, as a buyer or seller of a residential investment property, you will not be the one choosing the appraiser. The bank or lender has this privilege. Remember again, lenders are merely trying to protect themselves from doling out risky loans.

There is one way to completely avoid appraisers: by paying cash for a property and not even involving a bank or lender. Unfortunately, this is not the most efficient way of obtaining real estate, as you would not be using one of real estate's main advantages—leverage. This is not to imply that one cannot consider purchasing a property using all cash, but one's goals need to be evaluated when doing so.

How to Find a Good Appraiser

Even though during a transaction, you will rarely be the one choosing the appraiser, it is still a good idea to have, in your address book, one that you trust. It is the lender who usually chooses the appraiser; however, some lenders may be open to suggestions. This is when you want to throw in the name of your appraiser as a possible pinch-hitter.

Loan officers work closely with appraisers, so ask your loan officer for a referral. Also find out what the appraiser's turn-around time is. You don't want to wait weeks to get an appraisal. Remember that in any part of a real estate transaction time is of the essence. Ultimately, your loan officer should know who is fast and fair. Make sure that the appraiser has a good working knowledge of the local market. Experience in an appraiser is desired; however, it is not a useful gauge if he or she is difficult to get along with. An appraiser with a big ego is not likely to be flexible if a dispute in value arises.

Be careful not to break the law, as there a few appraisers willing to "sell" you the exact number that you are looking for. Don't get involved in this kind of exchange. Respect and honesty are essential when dealing with an appraiser. Even when the appraisal value is not exactly what you were hoping for, be respectful of their view. You can calmly discuss the disparity but treat them professionally.

Escrow/Title Company

Many people cringe when they hear the word *escrow* mainly because they don't understand what it means. This kind of fear can cripple even the best-intentioned investor. Escrow is actually quite straightforward and is a crucial process for the investor. It encompasses an entire centralized process for buying or selling a property. Ordinarily, when a contract is agreed on between a buyer and seller, money is given from the buyer to the seller in the form of an *earnest deposit*. This is usually anywhere from a thousand dollars to tens of thousands of dollars, depending on the price of the property, or roughly 1 percent to 3 percent of the asking price. It is applied to the purchase price of the house and is used to hold the property for the buyer. The seller or the seller's representative will then remove the property from the market pending the sale. In order to minimize exposure to fraud, loss, theft, error, or a conflict of interest, the earnest deposit is given to a third and neutral party called the escrow company. This company will then *open escrow* for the pending sale and hold the money until the transaction is completed or cancelled by both parties. The escrow company ultimately coordinates all of the necessary steps between the buyer and seller, from beginning to end.

In communities with a growing housing market, escrow companies are popping up left and right. The more experienced the escrow officer, the more likely your transaction will proceed smoothly. Technically, the buyer who makes the offer gets to select the escrow officer and title company handling the transaction. However, the seller can suggest a preference in a counter offer. So if you have the option, choose a company that is fairly established and has a good reputation among real estate agents.

Trusting the advice of real estate agents on this matter is useful because they usually have a fair amount of contact with escrow officers and companies. Some escrow companies will even give discounts to agents who bring in repeat business. Be aware that escrow representatives often give real estate agents small gift items in order to entice them to use their company. Most agents will not refer to these companies simply because of these gifts, but there will always be exceptions.

Do not allow escrow fees to be the main determinant when choosing a company. Look for quality first, as the escrow company can directly affect the timing and efficiency of a transaction. Since "time is of the essence" in any real estate transaction, it is usually a written part of the contract. Therefore, if the sale is not completed in a timely manner or by a certain date, the seller often has the right to cancel the contract and keep your earnest deposit. Because sellers have such control over the logistics and timing of the transaction, and timing is so important, the escrow company that you choose is also extremely important.

Something else to consider is that escrow is handled in very different ways in different parts of the country. For instance, in parts of the eastern section of the country, escrow is handled by lawyers, while in the West, independent escrow companies have free reign over this process. So find out which group will be in charge of escrow at the beginning of the process.

Finally, title is a part of the escrow process. When you purchase a property you will want to obtain a title policy. This policy protects you against any outstanding liens put against the property before your purchase but missed by a title search. Without title insurance, you could potentially be liable for other people's errors. Ultimately, the policy ensures that you will be the sole owner of the property. It is well worth the price of admission, so to speak. Oftentimes, the title company and the escrow company are one and the same.

How to Find a Good Escrow/Title Company

Title companies spend a good deal of their time soliciting business from real estate agents. Therefore, ask your agent which company has actually fulfilled its promises and which ones seem to create problems during closing transactions. If you are working with a Realtor®, use the title company and escrow officer that he or she recommends. After all, it is the agent who will constantly be in contact with the escrow officer during your transaction. The same criterion applies when you are working with a lawyer instead of an agent. Past experience and long-term relationships will generate more loyalty from the escrow officer than a one-time client will. By providing excellent and timely service, escrow officers build a reputation that allows them to attract more business. If you have many buying or selling transactions, try to stick with the same escrow officer. With an established and positive relationship, your requests will likely carry more weight than if you were a complete stranger.

Unfortunately, some title companies will not work with independent investors, while others offer special programs and discounts for investors. Many investors aren't aware of the fact that title and escrow companies compile very large amounts of data on their particular area. So ask your escrow officer about *farming* packets, which include demographic and other statistical information on a certain geographical area. The information is so detailed that they can pinpoint for you the name of every owner on a specific street or neighborhood that interests you. This information can be useful for the investor if he or she is creating mailing lists in order to farm a specific area. In this way, an investor can establish who the prospective buyers or sellers might be and act accordingly. This information is usually provided for free; the only catch is that some of the companies will only make these packets available to real estate agents. Search out those title companies that are willing to work with you as an investor because if they already have a negative view of investors, then any closing with them could be complicated and unpleasant. The bottom line is that communicating and building rapport is essential to obtaining quality service with a title company and their escrow officers. This should be a two-way street.

Real Estate Attorney

You may get great advice from real estate agents or brokers based on their experience, but proper legal advice is invaluable. Nothing can substitute for a true understanding of the law and how it is enforced. An attorney who specializes in real estate law can tell you what to expect during a legal dispute based on facts, not simply assumptions or guesses that your agent may provide.

Though others may offer you their opinion, ONLY a real estate attorney can give you reliable legal advice.

Obviously, no one wants to NEED a lawyer, so set up your investment team, entities, and advisors early in order to avoid this necessity. As discussed earlier, certain states (mainly in the eastern part of the country) require that escrow be handled by a lawyer instead of an escrow company. In most other states, if you purchase through a licensed agent, a lawyer is not necessary. However, in this litigious society, never say never! If something goes awry during a transaction, you may be the one who has to involve a lawyer for one reason or another, such as filing a lawsuit.

We strongly recommend using a real estate attorney, in any state, if you choose to buy or sell a property as a For Sale By Owner, also known as a FSBO (pronounced "fizbo"). You may even hire an attorney to prepare a sales contract prior to putting the house on the market or shopping to buy one. This way, you will be prepared for any questions from the new buyer. We also strongly recommend that you avoid simply using a generic sales contract form from a legal forms store when buying or selling a property. These forms are usually biased towards one party or the other and may carry less weight legally if there is a dispute in the future. Again, over-simplification will save you some money in the beginning, but can cost you significantly in the end. A reasonable fee for the lawyer's escrow service is approximately 1 percent of the sales price but can vary from locale to locale. So call around first and find out exactly what services a lawyer provides for his or her fees.

Remember that while there are many good and decent lawyers, every profession has its bad apples. We especially dislike lawyers who falsely instigate building-defect lawsuits in condominium projects, or ones who file bogus claims against HOAs on behalf of negligent renters. These lawyers and their lawsuits create a huge financial burden on the entire housing system in this country. They contribute greatly to the rising cost of insurance. They even affect the small investor. On the other hand, knowledgeable and honest real estate attorneys are well worth their fees when their participation frees you up for more productive activities. Just having an attorney backing you up on a transaction can create an air of legitimacy, forcing the other side to act legally and appropriately. Unfortunately, some people need the threat of legal action against them (a letter from your lawyer, for example) to do what is right. While it is preferable to hire an attorney who specializes in real estate, it is not mandatory. A general lawyer, as long as he or she is aware of any recent changes to the law, can take care of most of your real estate needs. Once you have found an excellent attorney, keep in touch with him or her, even if you do not have any legal issues at the moment. Eventually you will need their services. This same attorney can help you with a wide array of legal issues, from writing up a contract to helping with a nonpaying tenant to writing a letter to a noncompliant contractor. When you are face to face with a legal issue is not the time to be interviewing for a new lawyer. Have a lawyer in place and familiar with your situation long before you need his or her services. In a way, having a real estate attorney on the team is like having insurance. You hope that you will never need it but are glad that you do when the time arises.

Home Inspectors

Home inspectors can save you lots of time and money. For example, let's say that you recently got a property under contract to purchase, meaning that you put down a small amount of money (called an *earnest* or *good faith* deposit) to hold the property for you. In the contract your agent has included a clause stating that any forward motion is contingent on your inspection of the property. You get a professional inspector out to the property within a couple of days who finds that there are many not-apparent problems that could cost thousands of dollars to repair. Since your contract was contingent upon an acceptable inspection report, you are able to cancel the deal and retain your full earnest deposit. At this point, you should make sure to thank your agent for skillfully placing the contingency clause. In this case, the roughly three to four hundred dollars you spent on the inspector has saved you tons of wasted time and money.

Finding a Good Home Inspector

A good home inspector is very thorough. We've seen some get down on their hands and knees and crawl under places or climb up into the attic or even scale their way onto the roof in order to check every nook and cranny. This is what you are paying for. Before you choose an inspector, find out what is included in his or her fees and what type of training and experience the inspector has. If you have more questions, ask for references. A construction background is desirable but does not guarantee superior performance.

Once you have found a trustworthy inspector, use his services repeatedly. As a repeat customer, you will likely receive discounts. As a recurrent customer, you will also know that you can simply turn over the property to him and let him do his work. For a minimal fee, this team player can certainly add to your peace of mind.

On the first professional inspection that we personally witnessed, the inspector didn't even run the dishwasher to see if it worked. Therefore, for the first time or two you that you hire an inspector, stick around fairly closely for two reasons: first, to make sure the inspector actually does the job and second, to learn about inspections yourself. You can learn what common problems to look for when purchasing your next property.

Insurance Agent

This person will help you insure your properties in case of damage by nature, accident, acts of God, or your tenants (which unfortunately can seem like an act of God). Again, hopefully you won't need their services, but a good insurance agent and insurance company will know the best coverage for your situation and prepare you for major problems should they occur. Basically, there are three kinds of hazard insurance for your properties: an owner-occupied policy, a second-home policy, and an investment or non-owner occupied policy. In general, owner occupied and second-home policies will cost less because, based on their actuarial studies or statistics, the insurance companies can assume that you will take better care of your own house than a renter will take care of your investment property. Luckily for landlords, this isn't always the case, as long as the tenants are appropriately screened.

One often overlooked insurance policy is umbrella coverage. This policy will kick in after your car, life, or home policies have been depleted. So, if you ever get sued and have to pay some money, instead of having to liquidate your hard assets (such as cash, home, cars, or other real estate) the umbrella policy will pay out up to your policy's limit. This limit is usually in increments of one million dollars. Lawsuits making this type of policy necessary can be anything from someone slipping and falling on one of your properties to a lawsuit totally unrelated to your real estate. The charges may be frivolous but can cause a lot of financial damage if you are not protected appropriately. It is recommended that you obtain at least one million dollars of coverage when you are starting to invest. A $20 per month premium will provide you with plenty of security and peace of mind. A good agent can guide you to the right umbrella policy to fit your particular situation.

Again, in today's lawsuit-crazed environment, you have to think defensively and take the necessary precautions every step of the way or else you risk losing everything for which you have worked so hard. You might even think to yourself, "I'm very careful," or "I won't get sued." Unfortunately, it doesn't come down to how careful you are. Someone can simply create a frivolous lawsuit against you that can ruin your growing but humble real estate empire. All of this can occur as long as you do not have proper and adequate insurance coverage. As Ahmet's father likes to say, "The odds of something bad happening to you may be small, but when it does occur to you, the odds suddenly become 100 percent!" The results can be devastating and life-changing, so don't take that chance.

Eventually, if you own enough properties under a single limited liability company, or LLC (discussed later), you can obtain a commercial insurance policy. This can cost less money depending on the insurance company and can also be easier to manage for your business. In general, if you have most of your personal accounts with a particular insurance company, such as home, life, disability, or car insurances, they will be more likely to give you a discount for your investment properties.

When your property is rented, encourage, if not require, that your tenant purchase renter's insurance. It is an inexpensive policy that will protect renters' personal belongings from theft, damage, and other undesirable situations. The hazard insurance that you obtain for the property itself will not cover the tenant's belongings, so with renter's insurance in place, you should be off the hook if something happens to their belongings.

Insurance is one case when it is a good idea to shop around for the lowest price, assuming equal coverage. However, beware of the insurance sales ploy that will try to get you to buy more coverage than you actually need. Remember that insurance agents usually get paid by commission, so the more they sell to you, the more money they will make. Also, with more and more fraud occurring against the insurance companies themselves, they are more likely today to investigate and even deny certain high-risk claims. So it is important to evaluate an insurance company regarding how they handle customer service after a claim is actually filed.

However, unless you have already made claims through an insurance company for something, you won't have that direct experience. Therefore, ask friends and family if they have ever had to make a claim with their insurance company, and if so, was the company reasonable to deal with or was getting money out of them like going to the dentist and pulling teeth (i.e. *painful*)? As long as you are a reasonable risk to them, insurance companies will be more than happy to take your money for a new policy. However, when it is necessary to pay out for a claim, they can become like a dried-up lakebed and if the claim is a large one, then they may even cancel your coverage afterwards. For this reason, when considering filing a claim, unless you have a catastrophic or unaffordable situation, such as your property is destroyed by fire, etc., don't file it! Take the financial loss up to a personal bearable threshold. Why? As we just mentioned, insurance companies today are cancelling policies after a first claim. Unfortunately, they seem to have the law on their side and will probably continue with this practice.

How to Find the Right Insurance Agent

As usual, ask around. Ideally, you want to talk to someone who has made a claim with the company that you are investigating. This way, you'll find out how the company responds to a claim. Also, make sure that the company has a long history and a good reputation in the community. As long as the company has good standings in the financial world, based on ratings by Moody's or Standard and Poor, it will probably be around for a good long time. You don't want to give money to a company that suddenly disappears when you have to make a claim. Compare apples to apples. If there is a vast difference in premiums, there is probably a vast difference in what's being covered.

The agent represents his or her company. Your relationship with the agent is important over the long haul. Make sure that he or she understands the different needs of investment properties versus a personal residence. There are differences. The agent must be easy to reach in times of questions or need. Don't rely on the company's toll free number, as it will often be in another city and their representatives may not be very helpful. Ultimately, the agent should be responsible for directly answering any of your questions or problems.

It is also very important to remember that, each time you ask for an insurance quote, the insurance company will need to run your credit. This can adversely affect your Fair Isaac and Company (FICO) score. Therefore, try to keep the inquiries to a minimum, especially if you are in the process of getting a loan. Insurance policies can be easily changed, so there may be times it serves you to just go with a builder's company or someone you've used in the past just to get the loan closed. Afterwards, though, you can go ahead and switch the policy to a more favorable one. There are even special policies for furnished vacation rentals versus standard rentals, so make sure your policy matches your current needs.

Chattels Appraiser

The chattels appraiser is an integral part of your team for tax savings. However, as we mentioned earlier, the importance of the chattels appraiser is often overlooked. Why is it overlooked? Probably because most people don't want to pay the $300 to $400 fee—i.e., they are cheap and don't think it is worth it! Believe us, it is well worth it, especially if you are planning to buy and hold for several years or more. The $400 fee can save you thousands in taxes every year, not to mention the legitimacy it will carry with the IRS if you happen to be one of the approximately 1 percent of people who get audited each year.

When is the best time to get a chattels appraisal? Right away! Don't wait! The very BEST time to get a chattels appraisal is just after you purchase the home and fill it with appliances. This way you are not inconveniencing the new tenants. Also, if the renters have already moved in, the appraiser may not know who owns items such as the refrigerator and washer and dryer. So do it ASAP.

Ideally, your appraiser will take digital photos, use accurate digital measurements, and give you both the photos and the chattel values on a computer disk. This way you can either print out the appraisal to give to your accountant or send in the disk itself. Always keep a copy for your records.

There is one circumstance, though, that really does not call for a chattels appraisal: when you are simply selling a property within a few short months of its purchase, i.e. flipping the property. Because of the short period of ownership, you will not have much of a tax benefit to make it worthwhile.

Finding a Good Chattels Appraiser

This is not the type of vendor you will find in the yellow pages. Many people that you ask won't even know what chattels are because *chattels* is a business-specific term. Ask other seasoned investors to recommend someone. Definitely ask your CPA, since they should have seen reports from good chattels appraisers.

It is imperative that your chattels appraiser stay up to date with tax laws that pertain to these specific deductions. Don't try to do this one by yourself. The tax code is huge and you don't want to miss anything that can save you big money or deduct something that will raise a red flag for an audit.

Entity Experts for Corporations and Asset Protection

Because we live in such a litigious time in America, all real estate investors, small or large, must take the appropriate measures to protect their assets from frivolous lawsuits (there are also tax benefits with corporations). In general, the ideal goal for asset protection is to own nothing but control everything. Usually the actual circumstance may fall somewhere in between the two, depending on your personal situation. When initially considering asset protection, your most important team advisors to consult are your real estate attorney and your accountant. Consult them BEFORE you purchase any investments. They should have the knowledge to advise you in the various ways to hold real property and to differentiate between them.

Corporations provide legal protection by actually being the legal and recorded owners of a property instead of having the property be in your name directly. This separates your personal finances from your properties' finances. If you are protected in such a way and lose a lawsuit directed against you personally, then only your personal assets will be at risk, sparing all of your properties in the corporations from loss. The reverse holds true if one of your corporations loses a lawsuit. Again, if you are protected correctly, then only the holdings of that particular corporation will be affected and your personal assets will be spared from loss. Certainly, in most states, a lawyer could eventually legally uncover where all of your assets are hidden, but at least the corporation provides an initial layer of protection. As of the writing of this book two states, New Mexico and Delaware, will not make public the names of the corporate members or owners. To create the most security available, set up your corporations in one of these states. If you are looking for the lowest tax burden on corporations, then look into setting up your entities in states like Nevada or Wyoming. Again, talk to your advisor before making a move.

Today, limited liability companies, or LLCs, are very popular and effective entities for holding real estate investments. Ideally, you place only one property into each LLC that you create. However, this can become expensive. Therefore it is acceptable for small investors to initially put two or three properties in a single LLC.

During tax time, a limited liability company can act as a *flow-through* entity, meaning that any gains or losses from the properties in that LLC will actually flow through or be transferred to your personal tax accounting. As discussed earlier, since you will likely have a loss on paper with your real estate holdings in an LLC, this negative flow-through will help to offset any rental, W-2 or 1099 income that you have created. Again, real estate can legally reduce your tax burden greatly!

Now, the above is a highly simplistic view of asset protection. Other entities do exist, such as the C Corporation, the S Corporation, and the Limited Partnership. However, our above discussion of LLCs should provide you with a basic but very important understanding of the most appropriate entity for holding real estate. The actual legal use of an entity can be complicated and even change over time, so having an expert advisor in this field guiding you is necessary when looking for the best legal protection from lawsuits and taxes.

How to Find an Entity Expert

Make sure that a professional who is experienced in entities is the one who actually sets up your corporations. Otherwise, if you do it yourself or hire someone inexperienced and an error occurs, it could cause you months or even years of bureaucratic and IRS trouble. While the logistical process of creating an entity is not complicated and simply involves filing paperwork, unless you are experienced in this field, outsource it to the experts at least in the beginning. Better yet, don't be cheap. Leave it up to the professionals every time.

There are several team members, some already discussed, who can accomplish this goal. These include CPAs and attorneys, as well as companies that solely create entities as their main service. Make sure that whoever you choose for this task has experience in setting up corporations specifically for the small real estate investor! Cutting corners on this will only cost you more in the future. Unfortunately, all of this legal posturing is necessary just to protect your hard-earned investments from being taken in a lawsuit. Always use protection!

Spouse or Significant Other (S.O.)

This team member should actually be number one on *all* of our lists. Without your partner's support, the game is lost from the beginning and the journey is not worthwhile. Now, if you are single, you can either continue on or skip this section entirely, but for those it applies to…listen up.

Working with your spouse or S.O. can provide immense joy and stress. If you are both reasonable people and think in terms of working as a team, then not only can this process create more wealth, it can even bring the two of you closer. So form the foundation of a new and solid team. Promise to work through any disagreements before they get too big and keep talking about your goals and needs. With this open team approach, tasks can be split up, wins can be shared, losses lessened, and fortunes can be made together.

When tasks are split up, don't attempt to divide them 50/50. Instead, divvy them up according to each other's strengths. This will create a more efficient team. Take classes together and make plans together. Just like anything else in life, if you have a special person to share it with in a positive manner, then you will be much more likely to be happy and successful. And remember again that when it comes to this valued team advisor, don't be cheap. Pay your S.O.

well! Just kidding—well, sort of. Just as you would with your business cohorts, shower your spouse or S.O. with compliments, keep the criticisms constructive, and buy tons of gifts for him or her!

How to Find a Good Spouse

(Sorry, that's a different book.)

Frugality in Real Estate Investing

Okay, you might have recognized a recurring theme that has popped up after introducing each team member. If you didn't, then our writing style really bores you and you should stop, get some coffee, and reread this chapter. Anyway, we say "don't be cheap" for a reason. These team members will help you create and protect assets in very different but important ways. The general public has no second thoughts about tipping waiters or parking attendants. We tip these people because they provide a finite service to us but in no real way affect our financial lives. Don't get us wrong, we recommend that you continue tipping waiters and valets for excellent service but now also appropriately reward those people on your investment team. After all, what service could be more important than helping you to buy, manage, and sell assets that create wealth and security for you and your family? Wouldn't you be pleasantly surprised if one of your tenants paid you $100 extra one month in rent because they wanted you to know that you were a great landlord? I thought so.

Don't Sweat It

Don't sweat the small stuff in the beginning. For example, too many people get so caught up in the wording of a contract that they are ready to cancel a good deal over something that they never had control of in the first place. Again, a good team advisor will help you around such usually minor obstacles. Many broker, association, bank, and builder contracts are in standard form for that particular company. If something is stated or worded blatantly antagonistically and there is no way around it, then avoid the deal. However, most of the time, if the phrase in question is only slightly beneficial to the company and not you, either you will sign the contract or lose the deal. Don't try to change the institution's contract, as it is highly unlikely that you will come out the victor in this battle. And if you do win, it is likely that you will be scathed to the point that you will not be able to do the deal anymore. Even Donald Trump has to abide by some of these rules, although he has the clout to request changes and come out the unscathed victor. You are not Donald Trump...yet.

"Rich Dad®" Robert Kiyosaki likes to remind people that before you begin the investing game, you must first know what the rules are. These rules have likely been in force for decades and one person will not be able to alter them. Study and learn them so that you can take legal advantage of them. Our founding fathers set up the government in such a way that it assists people who want to become successful. So, read about and surround yourself with people who are already successful and absorb their information like a sponge.

But, again, don't get overly caught up in the details of the small stuff in the beginning. Understand as much as you can and listen to your team members when in doubt. Don't expect to know everything in the beginning. By looking at the big picture, you will allow yourself to learn the details over a period of time, making it a more manageable task.

Be thorough without being unreasonable. Real estate investing should be and can be a win-win situation for all parties involved, as long as no one gets greedy. However, since neither side of a deal is going to win all of the battles, know what is important to you and decide what you are willing to give up for it. Can't we all just get along? Sure, as long as no one is cheap—or greedy!

Not a Method but an Approach

Many of you may still be wondering when this book will cover specific techniques for buying the next deal. Well, as we told you in the beginning, that is not what this book is about. There are too many books that espouse the next surefire way of making a million in six months using real estate. These "experts" use arrogance and attitude to trick the general public into believing that using their so-called simple steps and methods will make you rich. This is grossly misleading and unfortunately, some of these self-proclaimed real estate gurus can now be found in court, jail, or on probation for fraudulent activity. So buyers, beware. Instead of losing your hard-earned money to these schemers, surround yourself with real experts.

Every investor needs to figure out what method works the best in their own location as well as for their own personality and preferences. Some of the methods taught today include preconstruction opportunities, lease options, preforeclosures, foreclosures, no money down, lots of money down, etc. Teaching you exactly what methods we used to make money is not efficient for you. After all, we are only one couple using certain methods. In order to prove that a particular technique really works, the results would have to be easily repeatable. This would require an extensive scientifically based study. If at all possible, remember to avoid trusting any single source for all of your information. You have to verify its truth or disprove it yourself. And since we have such a large country with multiple real estate markets that are influenced mainly by local economies, any one technique is bound to succeed or fail somewhere in the U.S. We believe that learning to build a team of advisors is a much wiser approach. Using a team of trusted advisors is a more efficient way to learn about your locale and exactly what method will best suit you and your investment needs.

Chapter 6

The Management Team

Some team members from the purchase will become regular players, while others will stay in the backfield temporarily, at least for this stage of the investing process. However, don't lose complete contact with these sidelined players, as most of them will need to return to the field during the next stage: selling. In the meantime, several new and important players will be drafted to add to your already important roster. Let the games begin!

So you've put your last signature on the loan documents and the property is now officially yours (and the bank's, of course). Now what do you do? You've got it…rent the darn thing! So numero uno on the list is learning about the new inductees into your growing hall of fame. They are:

1) Property management

2) Marketing connections

3) Certified Public Accountant or CPA

4) Bookkeeper

5) Banker

6) Home warranty company

7) General maintenance service

8) Landscaper or gardener

9) Pool service

Property Management

One could argue that this teammate should be consulted *before* any purchase because some key questions should be answered prior to buying a property. The main question being, "how will you get the place rented in the most efficient and profitable manner?" Also, who will be the property manager? For this last question, there are two simple options—either you (and/or your S.O.) or someone else. The tricky part of the question is that there is no right answer, as eventually you will need to learn the basics of property management anyway.

It comes down to asking yourself a few important questions. Are you physically capable of doing it? Do you want to do it? Do you mind driving across town if necessary, and if you live out of town, can you get there quickly enough in the rare case of an emergency? Usually your instincts will guide you to the right answer on this one. Some important factors to consider when making your decision include:

a) Location

Is the property nearby? Can you get there fairly easily if you are needed in a hurry? If the distance makes you uncomfortable, then you may want to start out with property management until you can under-stand the logistics completely. In the beginning of your investing career, it is recommended that you buy a property in an area that is easy for you to reach. So, ideally your first property would be within an hour or so of your home. This will allow you to gain valuable, first-hand experience in managing your property. This does not mean that you use this as your main buying criterion and purchase the house across the street! In fact, it is possible and recommended, at some point in your investing career, to incorporate investing in areas outside of your personal locale—but this is a subject for a future book.

b) Human Interaction

Conflict, unfortunately, is part of being a social society, and while most interactions with people are neutral or pleasant, there will be some conflicting relationships. If you are not comfortable or willing to deal with this, then by all means, hire property manage-ment because the conflict you will encounter may detract from the rewards inherent to real estate investing.

c) Time

This one is simple. Do you have the time? As long as your prop-erties are reliable, then the most time-consuming and expensive part of doing property management will be finding the right tenant. Once the tenants are in, then a single property will not be too difficult to manage by yourself. Unless, of course, your tenants are difficult, then all bets are off. This is why screening tenants is so important.

d) Money, Money, Money!

Of course, hiring a professional management company will eat into your cash flow. Good managers will spend a good deal of time running around dealing with unhappy (and happy!) people, some of them possibly your tenants. So, as with any frontline defense position, it can be a demanding job. Therefore, when you finally do find a good property manager...you've got it. Don't be cheap! Reward them well.

Ordinarily, for unfurnished rentals, property managers will charge a 10 to 15 percent fee for each month's rent that they collect for you. There may also be other one-time charges, for instance a percentage fee for finding each new tenant, i.e. a finder's fee. Furnished rentals, being much more time-intensive, fetch higher commissions of 20 to 25 percent of collected rents.

As you can see, the costs and fees can add up very quickly and cut into your cash flow, but on the other hand, having a property manager creates free time for you to use for sleeping, shopping, eating, playing, going on vacation, or yes, even working more. Not to mention that all costs related to property management are tax-deductible. So you will probably get back some of those expenses in the form of tax savings. With real estate investing and taxes, there is almost always a silver lining.

One point to remember is that no one will be a better property manager than you can be for your own properties, assuming that you are physically capable. Not Uncle Joe, Aunt Jenny, or Cousin Harry, no one. This is human nature, unfortunately. Unless someone has the most direct connection to a property, i.e. ownership, they will not care for it as well as you will. We won't say never or always, because there will be exceptions.

That being said, hiring a property manager can still be a very good move for you as long as steps are taken to monitor their actions. Do not find a property manager, hire them, and then expect that everything will be fine and completely hands-off. This may eventually happen, but at first, keep a close eye on their progress. Don't just open the yellow pages and find the best looking ad for property managers and hire one immediately. Just because they spend money on a pretty ad, doesn't necessarily mean that they will just as easily spend time and money on you and your property. Think about finding a manager like hiring someone to take care of your kids while you are gone on vacation. With this mentality, you will more likely find someone who will pay attention to details and understand your goals.

Don't just sign over the property and walk away. Periodically check on management if they are not already giving you status reports. Think about worst-case scenarios when hiring team members, and include, in contracts, clauses that will reasonably protect your interests while still allowing the team member to do the job that they were hired to do.

Even after you screen managers, you can still run into problems. Friends of ours, who for two years owned and managed furnished, short-term vacation rentals in Las Vegas, decided that it was time to hire property management. By doing so, they hoped to free up time to buy more investment properties. After doing some research, they agreed to hire a company on a two-month trial basis. (A full year is usually the standard length for a property management contract but both parties agreed to a two-month trial period.) The owner of the management company toured the properties and stated, because of the quality of the properties, that she should have no problems quickly renting them and also touted a "95 percent fill rate." The couple was ecstatic! The management company was hired on and all responsibilities were turned over to the new management. The couple anticipated their first rental check!

Once a week, the couple called the owner of the company and asked if he had rented any time in any of the three properties. Two months later, the property management had not even filled 1 percent of the openings, let alone 95 percent. They had not even booked a single guest! Furious, the couple opted out of their contract using their two-month trial clause and took back control of management. Within two days of work, the couple had booked thousands of dollars worth of rental time themselves. By adding the clause allowing them to cancel the contract after a trial period of two months, the couple saved themselves from losing tens of thousands of dollars in lost revenues had they depended on this inept management company. To this day, they are filling the property themselves, still wanting to turn over management to a deserving professional.

Other times, depending upon the investments you make, you may have put your money where you would never put yourself. Let us explain. A physician we know, who has dabbled in real estate, was commiserating with us about difficult tenants. We were telling him about how difficult it was to sometimes collect rent, even from otherwise good tenants. It turned out that he owned a four-unit apartment complex which he managed himself. His complex was in such a crime-ridden part of town that he had to take his gun with him to pick up the rent! We were flabbergasted.

Why would this educated person willingly put himself at risk every time he goes to pick up the rent? No cash flow is worth your life. Whether you are the property manager or you have hired someone else, don't put your life or another's at risk in such a manner. We strongly advise you to consider these issues when selecting your properties. Someone has to go there at some point. So, invest in safe areas that are pleasant to visit—there are a limitless number of such neighborhoods with investment opportunities. All you have to do is seek them out.

So You've Decided to Manage Your Own Investment Property

Basically, as property manager you will have many tasks before, during, and after renting a property. Below is a breakdown of those tasks in a simple timeline format:

1) Prepare the property to make it ready for tenants to move in.

2) Advertise it for rent.

3) Field all incoming calls.

4) Meet prospective tenants at the property. It is strongly recommended, for women especially, that you take along another team member or even a friend for safety and for legal reasons. You can't be too safe anymore.

5) Show the property.

6) Have prospective tenants fill out an application with or without collecting an application fee.

7) Run credit checks at home.

8) Check references.

9) And finally, if the moon and stars are aligned correctly, meet the new tenants at the property to collect rent and security deposit before they move in. Both must be received in the form of a cashier's check or money order. Personal checks are okay later.

10) Explain the lease contract, answering all questions.

11) Both parties sign the lease. Give the new tenants a copy with your signature on it for their records.

12) Hand over keys and garage door opener.

13) Congratulate yourself, go home, kick off shoes and have yourself a nice cold one! Oops, sorry, we are not done yet...

14) Follow up at the end of every month, with each tenant, in each property, to collect rent. Follow up on late payments, collecting any late fees or preparing eviction papers when necessary.

15) Repair or arrange repair of any items that are reported to you by tenants as soon as possible. Confirm with both the vendor and the tenant that the work was done satisfactorily, if not repaired by you.

16) Repeat steps 1 through 15 as necessary.

As you can see, this property management thing can be a busy day of running around. Plus, if you have multiple properties, while you are working with the prospective tenants at one unit, you may have to put out a fire or two at one of the other rentals. So when you read a book saying that real estate investing can be done "in your free time" or "part time," we recommend that you throw that book away (and read ours again)! If you hope to do things with respect and integrity, then true real estate investing will be a time consuming affair, as well as potentially profitable and enjoyable. Just be realistic about the amount of work and time that it really takes to succeed in real estate.

Another important aspect of management is providing the lease contract. Whether you or the management company provides the contract, time should be spent ensuring that there are adequate clauses protecting you, as the owner, in different circumstances. Since real estate laws differ throughout the country, it behooves you to talk to your upstanding real estate lawyer before using a particular lease contract. Ideally, you should read multiple sample contracts and use bits and pieces to suit your own needs. Over time, any sections that are outdated can be removed, while new sections are added. Once you have a rock solid lease agreement, you can use it for many properties. Check in with your attorney periodically to see if any changes in the law require altering your lease agreement, because city, state, and federal laws can change regularly. If you use a bad lease (i.e. outdated, undefined, etc.), then all your hard work could be undone in one fell swoop.

A Word about Tenants and Rents

Keep rents reasonable and within the local range. If you price rent too high, you will have a property that will stay empty. Instead, if a property is not moving, offer it for slightly below the market price. This way you will at least get some rent ASAP to cover the mortgage. Generally, it is better to rent for less than to leave a property empty for another month. The only time that it is preferable to leave a property empty is when the prospective tenant is potentially troublesome. Renting to a high-risk tenant will cost more in the long run than paying a month's mortgage without a tenant.

Court good or low-risk tenants. Instead of nickel-and-diming a prospective desirable tenant with an application fee, or other fees, tell them that because they were so nice you will apply those fees to the first month's rent or waive them altogether. This gesture will be appreciated and noted.

When your desired tenant has moved in and is paying rent on time, reward them. Around the holidays, or better yet at random times once or twice a year, send your favorite tenants a $10 to $25 dollar gift certificate to a local grocery store. This will let them know that you appreciate them for taking care of your property.

Because most tenants don't expect this kind of thoughtfulness from landlords, a little kindness will usually go a long way.

There are also ways to thank your tenant while simultaneously increasing the value of your property. For your best tenants in properties that have older appliances, think of offering the tenant a new appliance of their choice. This way, you have rewarded the tenant while replacing an appliance that would have broken down eventually. By not waiting until something does go wrong, you'll be perceived as a dream landlord instead of a slumlord. Now this is what we call good public relations!

Marketing Connections

Although it may depend on where you live, you may want to cozy up with someone in the classifieds department at your local newspaper. The best exposure and most efficient use of marketing money for your property is usually found in your local newspaper's rentals ads. Of course, this is assuming that your paper has a reasonably large circulation. Making this contact may seem silly, but it will enable you to learn about special deals that the newspaper offers or the best times to advertise in special supplements.

Another good and inexpensive method to advertise your unit for rent is by placing so-called *bandit signs*. These are homemade signs that you place on light posts, fences, bus stops, or other places with good visibility and high traffic. Use a brightly colored paper like yellow or orange and place the signs in clear plastic sleeves to protect against the elements. Otherwise, your sign may be gone in a matter of days (instead, let's hope your property will be gone or rented in a matter of days!). Put only basic info such as "House for Rent," the price, number of bedrooms, and your phone number.

Too much information can make it difficult to read and ultimately useless. Use only black or blue magic marker for better visibility. Make sure to place them in areas near the property but not on private property without permission. They are called bandit signs because they are usually put up in public areas very quickly, without formal approval. We do not advocate putting them up illegally if your local government does not allow them.

Nothing can take the place of a simple sign in the front yard or window of your property. People passing by already know if they like the neighborhood and what is nearby. Again, less is more with these signs. Just make sure that you can make out the phone number from the street. If they want to know more, they will call. However, they will never call if they know that it has three bedrooms and a pool, but can't read the last digit of the phone number. An illegible sign might as well not be there. It is amazing how many of these illegible signs we see all over the country.

Certified Public Account (CPA)

The amazing thing about real estate investing is that at a certain level of ownership and income, you will legally pay virtually no taxes. By hiring the right CPA for your situation, you can pocket thousands of dollars instead of paying it in taxes. A knowledgeable accountant will know the where, when, why, and how of tax deductions. The accountant you hire must have ample experience with real estate investors. Also important is that he or she always continues to stay on top of changes to the tax code. Each year may not see a Congressional overhaul to the internal revenue code, but there will be numerous court rulings, throughout the year, that can affect the way you and your CPA will account for items and deductions.

As the investor, you must have some basic knowledge about tax deductions and be able to apply them throughout the year. This is not something that you can do just before April 15. Your accountant is there to suggest legal ways to save money and to ensure that everything is accounted for correctly as you go along. It is much easier to keep track of potential deductions as they occur than it is to go back through twelve months of receipts just before tax time. Even if the internal revenue code gives you hives, you must learn some basics as it is an easy way to save money—and sometimes not as complicated as you might think.

How to Find a Good CPA

This is a time when you must know someone who already knows this team member because you will be giving this person all of your private financial information. It must be safe in this person's possession. Definitely interview an accountant to get a sense of his or her experience with real estate investments. Does he own any investment properties himself? If the answer is no, then you will probably want to keep looking. You don't have to have the same financial goals, but your CPA must be able to see the wisdom in real estate investing or else how can he or she help you? If the CPA too owns investment property, he or she will likely be on the lookout for the best and most up-to-date deductions. Even an initial $100 consultation fee is worthwhile if it saves you from hiring the wrong accountant for your situation. An audit is not the time to find out that your CPA is not an expert when it pertains to real estate investing and taxes.

Your personal time with a CPA is not extensive so you don't have to love his or her personality, but you will need someone who can translate your finances into IRS-friendly numbers and then back again. Remember that you are trusting this person to be able to legally back up everything on your tax return. Of course, this assumes the information that you provide them is accurate in the first place—thus the importance and need for organized and precise record keeping.

Bookkeeper

The bookkeeper is probably the one person who will be most often involved with your day-to-day transactions and record keeping. An experienced one will guide you if you do not have any bookkeeping experience and will be willing to take the time to educate you. Your life around April 15 of every year will be made much more enjoyable and easier with an experienced bookkeeper. By mulling through financial statements on a monthly basis with your bookkeeper, you will stay on top of your property's performance (or lack thereof) and be able to administer a solution, if need be, in a timely manner. In other words, large losses can be averted with appropriate bookkeeping. Remember, if you view your real estate investments from a business perspective, you will likely be more successful and in control of your wealth.

How to Find a Good Bookkeeper

Look around, ask around, and go through a few if necessary in order to find someone that you personally get along with, because you will be spending a good deal of time with your bookkeeper on a regular basis. It may also be of benefit if the bookkeeper's office is physically close by so in-person meetings can be easily arranged with little prior notice. Also, seeing the numbers yourself may be helpful in understanding the entire process.

Once again, a bookkeeper who has experience with accounting for investors is essential. This person does not have to personally own any properties, but must have worked on the books of other investors. Do not be his or her first client who's a real estate investor.

Oh yeah, one more thing: don't be cheap! Don't hire someone just because he or she charges the least. Hire a bookkeeper because the person seems to be experienced, helpful, and a good fit. As long as the bookkeeper is good at her work, don't worry if she charges slightly more than the other bookkeepers around. You will save money in the long run by not being frugal with this advisor.

Your accountant may work with a particular bookkeeper or have a relationship with a bookkeeping company. It's a good place to start the search. Ultimately, remember that the bookkeeper's office will have immediate access to plenty of your personal information, such as bank account numbers. So make sure that all references speak to the bookkeeper's honesty.

Banker

Get to know a bank teller, or better yet, a bank manager, in the bank branch that you use the most. Obviously, real estate is driven by financial matters, and money for good deals may be needed in a hurry. A friendly bank teller or manager can help you with a cornucopia of daily transactions and processes such as notarizing documents, depositing checks (especially large ones which can require a long hold before availability), or simply wiring money. Their services can be very useful.

Building good rapport with a bank manager can be very advantageous as they often have the authority to bypass certain bureaucratic steps that other bank employees cannot. Also, banks have their own grading system for each customer, so as your grade increases, so does your ability to do business in a more efficient and beneficial manner.

For example, during a trip to Washington, D.C., a deal which we had been working on for several weeks happened to require immediate attention back home. The seller of the property in question needed money wired to his bank within twenty-four hours or the deal would be cancelled. What bad timing to be away from home. Because there were no branches of our bank in D.C., none of the other banks could help us. So we called our bank manager friend back home as a last resort and he was able to wire the money from our account within one hour! Without this teammate, the property, and its equity of at least $50,000, would have been lost.

Think of all the time that you can save, from standing in line at the bank filling out paperwork, with the help of your own personal banker. It's probably safe to assume that Mr. Trump gets first class treatment through the back door of his bank.

How to Find a Good Banker

If you do all of your personal and business banking in one place, chances are you already recognize a few friendly faces. Introduce yourself and spark up a friendly conversation. Sincerely complimenting them on something can create a positive and lasting impression. Also make sure that you introduce yourself to the branch manager. Make an appointment to do this if necessary, but don't take up too much of their time as they are busy people. By doing so you are not asking for anything illegal, but it helps the bank manager to put a face with a name (or account number, in this case). Briefly explain your business and banking goals during a time that you do not need any assistance. This way, when the time comes when you do need some help, he or she will at least recognize you and remember how nice you have been.

Home Warranty Company

Things break down, that's a fact. That's why it is advisable that you buy goods and service of at least midland quality. Avoid the extremes of low end or high end (unless of course your property is high end). Buying at least decent quality goods and services will save you money in the long run.

However, realize that even expensive, high-end products can malfunction and require repair. Therefore, it is strongly recommended that, whenever you buy an investment property, you purchase with it a home warranty. This warranty is a contract with the company stating that if anything covered in the contract malfunctions, they will send out the appropriate professional (i.e. plumber, electrician, handyman, etc.) to attempt a repair for a standard and predetermined price (e.g. $45). If the repairman cannot repair the product, they will replace it at no extra charge.

How to Find a Good Home Warranty Company

During the purchase of a property, a good real estate agent should ask you whether you want a home warranty. In fact, many brokerages have their own affiliated warranty company or at least do business with a few. Again, as with insurance policies, compare apples to apples and make sure you know what systems in the house are covered with your premium. Get quotes from at least two different companies. Also ask your real estate agent if other clients have been satisfied with the company's response and service to their claims. It is generally a good-value service; however, some companies are better than others so ask around. Like any other insurance company, they will easily take your premium payment but getting a company to pay out on your own claim can sometimes be challenging. Hoping to avoid replacing a costly product, they may repeatedly get an item to work temporarily (without actually correcting the main problem itself) until it completely breaks down. Therefore, know the specifics of your policy and read the fine print.

General Maintenance Service

Now that you have a warranty in place, you will have no maintenance issues, right? Wrong! Over time, gather the names and numbers of a good plumber, electrician, handyman, carpet company, painter, etc. While a home warranty may be good for certain services and circumstances, you will want several layers of service as back up. If the home warranty does fail you, with these back-up or second-string team players, you will have someone available to take care of minor and major emergencies.

When the air conditioner stopped working completely, at the height of summer, in one of our Arizona rentals, we called the home warranty's emergency hotline. Unfortunately for us and our sweet, elderly, and disabled tenant, it was a weekend. The warranty representative on the hotline stated that because her computer showed Phoenix as having a current temperature of "only 85 degrees Fahrenheit," she could not mark it as an emergency! My blood started to boil and I became furious. "Of course it's 85 degrees, it's only 8:00 A.M., but the temperature is going to reach 108 today, according to the local forecast!" I bellowed. Then I asked, "What temperature does it have to be before it becomes an emergency?" The rep, in her air-conditioned office in Connecticut, responded rudely, "more than 85 degrees!" As you can imagine, we didn't get anywhere with this so-called customer service rep, who happened to also be the supervisor that day. So what happened to our little old lady tenant? Well, since the home warranty refused to get someone out until Monday, and it was still early Saturday, we had someone of our own choosing come out. It turned out that the entire AC unit was defective and needed to be replaced. Well, $4,000 later, our sweet, elderly woman was enjoying cold air from the new AC. But the battle with our warranty company had just begun.

That following Monday, we called the warranty company's sales representative, who had sold us the warranties for all six of our rental properties. After all, she was still getting a commission from these policies, and we figured that she might take some interest in our problem. As it turned out, the company did not even use temperature to determine whether or not there exists an emergency during an air conditioner failure. That determination is made by whether that malfunctioning AC is the *only* cooling unit available for the property—and in our case, it *was* the only unit. So, by getting the sales representative involved, we got the company to ultimately pay for the bill. Victory was ours, but it was hard fought.

As you can see, home warranty companies do not always immediately do what they are supposed to. This is why it's a good idea to have either the know-how to repair things or better yet, the name and number of some good and honest technicians in your area. They are your emergency response team!

If you are the property manager, then you will be, in all reality, the first exposed layer to any problem, while the second layer is the home warranty and the third and final layer will be the individual technicians.

At some point, you will want to leave town or take a vacation without having to worry about being on call for your real estate empire. In order to prepare for such an eventuality, start talking to other real estate agents, property managers, or even a trustworthy friend about possibly fielding any emergency calls should they occur while you are away, however unlikely. You can prearrange a stipend for their hard work as well as offer them great appreciation for allowing you to take time off from work.

If you only own one or two investment properties, then this is likely a moot issue. However, with more properties, the likelihood of something going wrong while you are away increases significantly. In this case, seriously consider hiring someone while you are gone. Arrange it well before your departure date to your dream vacation.

Remember that the best offense is still a good defense. With all the right people in place ahead of time, you will have done everything you can to prepare and prevent any problems from occurring or becoming out of hand. Then, if and when a minor emergency occurs, the team will respond accordingly.

How to Find Good Repair People

Reputation can be everything. Hold on to the names and numbers of vendors that you hear complimented by others. Even when you don't think you will ever need a good tile person, write their name and number down when a neighbor mentions them. If a lawn in your neighborhood looks particularly nice and well kept, find out who their lawn service is. Always be on the lookout. If you hire someone to repair your own house and they do a good job, keep their card for the future. Realtors® and property managers will have their own list of names. Depending on the city or town that you are in, businesses often come and go very quickly. Take note of the ones with a long local history and also those that give references. Check with your local contractor's board to see if a business has had any complaints against them.

A word of caution on "good" references from your chamber of commerce: vendors often pay to be recommended members. So, instead, go by personal recommendations from team members that you already trust. Finally, if at all possible, choose vendors who are licensed with your local government as well as insured and bonded. This way, if something goes awry, you will have the backing of their insurance company as well as the local government.

Below, we give special mention to a few particular vendors because of their common usefulness. Many people believe that they may be unnecessary, but we strongly recommend keeping their services handy and active.

Landscaper or Gardener

Landscaping will be the very first thing that a prospective tenant (or prospective buyer) will see when viewing your property, so make a good first impression. Of course, if you are renting out a condo or a townhome, the home owner's association is in charge of yard maintenance and you don't have much control. However, you can still place some real or fake potted plants at the doorway for a good impression; assuming your Conditions, Covenants and Restrictions (CC&Rs) allow it, of course. If you are renting out a house, make it appealing but don't go overboard unless it is a high-end rental and prospective tenants expect it.

Many real estate investors recommend that you write a clause in the lease contract describing, in detail, the tenant's responsibility when it comes to yard maintenance. This is great in theory, but oftentimes the tenant still won't take care of the yard and you'll end up paying loads of money to repair any damage with little financial recourse. Occasionally, though, you will get a tenant with a green thumb who makes the yard look like a botanical garden. As discussed earlier, reward these kinds of tenants. It is preferable, however, to err on the side of caution and to assume that your tenant will not care for the yard very effectively. The cost of hiring a monthly landscaper will usually outweigh the cost of replacing and repairing dead lawn, plants, bushes, and trees at the end of a tenant's term. If you do decide to have the tenant care for the yard, keep a close eye on it by driving by on a regular basis. It's a good idea to take a few photographs of the yard as well as the inside of the house. This way, in case you need to prove neglect or any violation of the contract, you will have proof in the form of before-and-after pictures.

Many gurus who teach lease options and rent-to-own as investment methods say that with these techniques, the tenants will be "motivated" to care for your lawn, yard, and house better than if they were simply renting. According to this theory, because they have a potential stake in future ownership, they will be more mindful of upkeep and maintenance. Unfortunately, human nature is usually such that unless someone actually legally owns something, he or she is much less likely to treat it as well as their own. Sometimes, even ownership does not guarantee good care! It all comes down to an individual's own values.

So don't assume that someone else will care for your belongings as well as you will just because someone told you in a seminar or you read it in a book. Remember to go out and verify or disprove questionable statements. In fact, don't believe anything that you read in *this* book unless you verify or disprove it yourself. Use this book only as a guideline.

Pool Service

Pools and spas can be large investments that add a fair amount of appeal to your property. Because of their hefty price tag to repair or replace, make sure that they are maintained. Just as with the yard maintenance, if you insist on having the tenant care for the pool, put it in the contract.

We prefer to hire and pay a professional pool-maintenance service in order to ensure that our investment is properly taken care of. Incorporate this cost into the rent if necessary or use it as an advertising draw: "Free Pool Service with One Year Lease." Don't rely on this, but the pool service can be another pair of eyes to alert you to backyard problems that you may not be aware of otherwise. Use every resource available to you in order to care for and maintain your investment property. It will ultimately be worth your time and money.

Chapter 7

The Sales Team

✳ ✳ ✳

Congratulations! At this stage you are ready for the big payoff. As a successful manager and business owner, you've become a regular Trump Jr.

Thinking First about What Comes Last

Every time you purchase a real estate investment, it's an excellent idea to think about your exit strategy for this particular property. In other words, consider how and when you plan to part with the property or "exit" this investment. Ask yourself how long you plan to keep this property: one, five, ten, fifteen, twenty years or longer. Or do you plan to sell it within the first few months of ownership? Are you deciding based on a time period or profit margin? Will you sell the property to pocket the booty or do you plan to defer your tax liability by entering into a 1031 exchange? (We will cover this later.)

Before the purchase, ask yourself if you plan on renting the unit furnished or unfurnished. Will you consider short-term rentals (less than six months) or even month-to-month rentals? Most of these topics won't be covered in this book with much detail. However, they are questions to seriously ponder before a purchase. This way, if you plan to sell in year five, you can always be applying certain tax benefits accordingly. Anticipation based on research and planning is a great tool for use in real estate investing.

Exit strategies, however, are not carved in stone. They should be used as basic guidelines. For instance, let's say that you purchase a beautiful property that you plan to hold onto for ten years, then 1031 exchange the profit into another investment property. Unfortunately, in year eight, the local economy starts to take a dive, driving housing prices down with it. Now it looks like you will be left with much less equity at the end of year ten than you originally expected. In this case, your original and reasonable strategy was derailed by the economic downturn. So in this example, don't feel obligated to stick with your original plan of selling the property in year ten, as it will likely yield little profit. Instead, extend and alter your exit strategy to fit these local market changes.

Even though your original exit strategy was based on the local conditions at the time of the purchase as well as the future forecast, most of us cannot see into the future. Predictions and projections can be inaccurate. *The only way to know what the future holds for us is to experience it.* So have a master plan for each property, but remain flexible to unforeseen changes. If there are no unforeseen changes then continue on your original path towards wealth.

Flexibility is another very valuable tool. Without it, you will likely lose many good opportunities and team members along the way. The team members you assemble should also know how to adapt to seen and unforeseen changes. So, even if the final goal is altered in some way, your relationship with team members should continue and even become stronger. Remember that in team sports, good leaders know how to alter plans according to the score.

Real Estate Agent

They're baaaack! Remember that during the purchase section you researched agents and found yourself a very honest and effective one. You may have gone through a few to find this gem, so use this agent to sell your property, if at all possible. Use the agent's services again especially since you trust this person and he or she probably already knows the area, as well as the property, very well. Oftentimes agents are viewed as generalists, meaning that they can help you in both transactions: buying as well as selling. If it turns out that the agent you used to purchase the property is strictly a buyer's agent, then ask him or her for a recommendation to a good listing or seller's agent. Sincerely compliment your agent by asking for a recommendation of someone who is as good as he or she is.

Since there are slightly different skills involved with selling a property, it is a wise decision to try and find someone who specializes in just selling real estate instead of both. When ultimately deciding on an agent, weigh the agent's familiarity with the property and the neighborhood; experience in sales; and network of other agents—which is crucial for getting the word out about your property.

As with the original purchase, an expert agent will save you time, energy, hassles, and yes, even money. Not to mention, again, that the agent and his or her broker will provide you with a legal layer of protection should something about the transaction be questioned in the immediate, near, or far future. Despite what many FSBO experts claim, the entire process of buying or selling a property on your own (i.e. without a lawyer or a real estate professional) is not nearly as easy and straightforward as they would like you to believe it is. In fact, even though Sheri is a great Realtor®, when we sell our own properties, we often use another agent for the reasons outlined above, especially for that extra legal layer of protection. And the one time that we actually did sell a property as a FSBO, we contracted a lawyer before placing the property on the market. It turned out that his fees were worth every dollar, as the buyer tried to unlawfully cancel the transaction. Luckily, with our attorney's help and Sheri's knowledge of the selling process, we were able to save the deal. So kudos to good Realtors® and good lawyers!

The Headaches of FSBOs

In certain market conditions, such as a seller's market, when houses and condominiums are a hot commodity and sell within days of listing, you may be tempted to do things yourself and sell your investment property as a FSBO. This way, you think you will be saving tons of money by not paying an agent's commission or a lawyer's fee. Well, stop and repeat after me...don't be cheap! This is not said just to put money into an agent's hand. It's true that you might, and we do mean might, save small amounts of money by not hiring an agent, but it is not worth it. With a FSBO, your expenses for simply marketing your property can be greater than what an agent pays to promote their entire portfolio of properties. In addition, the work of following up with buyers, qualifying them, opening escrow, tracking the transaction, etc., all still has to be done correctly and efficiently. Unless you are an agent or experienced in real estate transactions, it is well worth hiring an agent to do all of this for you, especially if you have another full- or part-time job. Real estate agents really earn their commission with all of the tasks that are required of them behind the scenes. Remember, don't be cheap! Hire a pro to do a professional job. And if you decide to ignore our advice, then at least hire a trusted lawyer to handle the legalities of the transaction.

Unless you are a trained real estate professional or have years of experience with FSBOs, you won't know what pitfalls to look out for. Real estate agents actually pay error and omissions (E&O) insurance out of each commission check to their broker. In turn, the broker carries an insurance policy that covers all of his or her agents. The insurance company will pay for wrongdoing or negligence that is found to be the responsibility of the agent involved with the transaction. Without this insurance policy during a FSBO transaction, if you sell a property and an irregularity is discovered later on, you will be personally responsible and liable for any damages in a lawsuit. This could end up costing you thousands upon thousands of dollars just in legal fees, not to mention lost time. If you don't think that these incidences can occur to you, just ask your agent to show you the industry rap sheet.

Doing a transaction in this manner is akin to a surgeon performing surgery without malpractice insurance, which is not a likely scenario in today's world of medicine. You should be constantly procuring ways of protecting yourself and your assets.

Certified Public Accountant

Consulting your CPA well before you sell a property can save you thousands of dollars in taxes around tax time. In general, if you hold a property for less than one year, it will be considered regular income by the IRS and will be taxed at your normal tax rate for the year. If you hold the property for at least one year and one day and then sell, your profit will be considered a capital gain and taxed at a capital gains rate of 5 percent or 15 percent (the exact rate depends on your earned income for that year). For many investors, 15 percent will be a much lower tax hit than their normal tax rate on earned income. Therefore, if at all possible, hold on to your investments for at least one year and one day before you sell them.

If you reach that one-year-and-one-day milestone, certain costs can legally decrease your profit on paper, thus further reducing your tax burden. While you are buying, managing, and selling properties, your first-rate tax accountant will be staying abreast of any and all pertinent government rulings and tax law changes that can affect your investments. This is why your accountant is so important and why you should always keep him or her informed of any major status changes. Your CPA can help you enjoy the profits rather than handing them over to the government. Eventually, you may have to pay the government a small portion of your profits in taxes. However, by that time you will have accumulated such a large fortune that giving away a small percentage won't hurt as much! After all, it is the very system that will allow you to accumulate this wealth. Until that day, though, there are ways to legally delay paying any taxes on your profits, thus allowing you to grow your profits bigger and faster. For example...

1031 Exchanges and the Qualified Intermediary

Before selling any investment property, there are two terms that you must learn and understand: 1031 exchange and qualified intermediary (QI). Once you actually utilize these fantastic tools, you will wonder why they are not household phrases! Without getting into boring legal specifics, a 1031 exchange is the section in the tax code that allows you to use the equity from one investment property to buy another investment property. All of this can be done without any, yes any, tax consequences to your equity. It legally allows you to defer paying taxes. Ultimately, 1031 exchanges allow you to have more capital to invest in multiple or larger properties, which in turn will bring larger returns in cash flow, appreciation, and tax deductions.

There are no limits to how many times you can 1031 exchange your equity. However, if you eventually do sell a property and pocket the profits, then you will have to pay taxes on those profits at that time. Hopefully by that time the equity will be so large that you really won't mind paying a small portion of it to the IRS. You don't mind sharing, right?

Once you have sold the subject property in a 1031 exchange, you have *exactly* forty-five days to identify a replacement property and a total of *exactly* 180 days to complete the transaction from start to finish. If you go one day beyond either deadline then the transaction is null and void. If this occurs, you will personally pocket all of the profits from the sale, and you will ultimately be visited by the tax man. Don't kid yourself into thinking that you can get an extension on a 1031 exchange if needed. Since the inception of the 1031 exchange, there have only been a few extenuating circumstances that forced the IRS to grant an extension: one of them was for September 11, 2001. In other words, be on time during this process.

The qualified intermediary is trained to help you in a 1031 exchange. In fact, the IRS mandates that a qualified intermediary be used during this process. This entity will serve as the possessor of the funds between transactions. Regardless of the reason, if any part of the equity reaches you or your bank account, even for a second, then you will have to pay taxes on it and the 1031 exchange is disqualified by the IRS. You may, however, designate a portion of equity to go towards a 1031 exchange while the remaining amount goes in your pocket as a profit. The only difference here is that the amount going to your pocket, also called *boot,* will get taxed accordingly. As you can see, because the government requires it, and because 1031 exchanges have many rules and regulations that must be followed, a knowledgeable qualified intermediary is an absolute must-have team advisor.

With real estate booming in various locales, many qualified intermediaries are popping up. And depending on your state, there is little to no governmental supervision of qualified intermediaries. As a result, many of them are not truly qualified and are set up only to take your money and then close up shop, never to be heard from again. In other words, these people can steal your hard-earned money and you will have little or no legal recourse to recover it. This is why it is so important to have at least a basic understanding of any investment process and to know exactly what each advisor is supposed to be doing. Without this critical knowledge, certain red flags and danger signals during a transaction can be easily missed. So, stick with qualified intermediary companies that are relatively large and have multiple branches throughout the country. This will strongly suggest that they are legitimate. Additionally, do as much research to verify their legitimacy as you reasonably can before you sign on the dotted line. This team member can win or lose the championship series for you. So choose carefully.

Because there are too many important details to fit in this book regarding the 1031 exchange, be sure that you consult with both your CPA and the qualified intermediary before making any game-deciding plans.

Tenancy-In-Common

A relatively new investment vehicle for real estate is the tenancy-in-common (TIC). This method involves real estate investment professionals who gather multiple investors to purchase a single commercial property. The company arranges all of the logistics of the purchase while the investors provide the capital. After the purchase, the company will also provide property management. Usually, the company looks to accumulate enough investors to cover approximately 40 percent to 60 percent of the purchase price, allowing for a low monthly mortgage (called *debt-service* in commercial lingo) and a high return for its investors. Even more recently, it has become legal to 1031 equity from a property into a tenancy-in-common. However, as with any other deal, you need to look at the actual financial numbers of the property to make sure that it is a good investment and that the company is legitimate.

Talk to other investors who are participating in or have participated in a tenancy-in-common. Get their feedback regarding the services that they have received from the company and the quality of the properties that were purchased by the company. Look at the company's past performance and be wise before buying.

Chapter 8

Keeping Your Sense of Humor

O ne thing we have not yet mentioned is the importance of having a sense of humor during your investing career. Though at the time we didn't necessarily think that some experiences were particularly funny, we can now look back and smile or even laugh out loud. Hopefully, the following stories will do the same for you, while reinforcing some important ideas.

Even with all of the best planning in the world, real estate investing is full of surprises. That's why it is so nice to have a team and not be alone out there. Your trusted team of advisors can help you when someone throws you an occasional curveball.

Replanting Hilltop Garden

Being somewhat handy with small power tools and hammers, we can repair certain minor items in and around a house. Despite this, we have not yet invested in a "fixer-upper"—at least not on purpose. One of our first deals was the purchase of a 2,300-square-foot house on Hilltop Garden Drive, a quiet street in a desirable neighborhood. The owner was looking to sell quickly, so he priced the house at $229K, which was low according to our agent's comparative research. Based on our professional inspection, we also knew that the house was in very good condition. Because we knew it was a deal, we wanted to make a very attractive offer that would not likely be refused. So we offered $239K, $10K over the asking price. Needless to say, our offer was accepted and we bought the property. Were we crazy? Wait and see.

Our exit strategy was to hold on to the property for at least five years, so we immediately began looking for a tenant. However, during this time, the rental market was soft, especially with this size of a house and its higher-than-average rent. Normally, as discussed earlier, we screen our own prospective tenants, but after a few months of not being able to rent the house, we enlisted the help of a rental service that finally got us a tenant. The people at the service were the ones who actually did the screening. Their job was simply to find us a decent tenant who was willing to pay the rent. Of course, with rental services, their commission is more of a motivator than is their desire to find a decent and qualified tenant for us. Nonetheless, we were assured that this person was well qualified, and because we were fairly desperate, we accepted the tenant for a twelve-month lease.

For the next year, Michael paid his rent, albeit usually late, and appeared to care for our property. At the one-year mark, he gave his thirty-day notice to leave but stated that his girlfriend would like to stay on for another year. After a brief screening process, we determined that Jennifer was a reasonable risk and so a new lease was signed. After all, she was already paying half the rent up to now. Everything looked just peachy keen until two months into her lease when Jennifer called and sobbed that she could no longer afford the rent. She wanted to cancel her lease. By this time, the rent was already five days late! No matter what the outcome, she was still legally responsible for paying the rent on the remaining ten months of the lease.

Unfortunately, it turned out that when Jennifer called us, she had already moved out, leaving behind a trail of destruction inside and outside of the property. What we encountered in that house was absolutely grotesque! The minute the front door opened, a stench of feces hit us like a ton of bricks. Jennifer apparently had two large Akita dogs who had not been approved by us. She allowed them to urinate and defecate inside the house on the carpet and tile. The carpet was trashed and had to be replaced even though it was only two years old. The entire house had to be repainted. Even the entire backyard landscape had to be redone, as she had managed to kill nearly every living thing that was planted. All this in two months!

You might have suggested going after her in small claims court. Unfortunately, the damage was over $10,000 (too much for small claims court), and she skipped town. Even if we had found her and took her to court, it would be like squeezing blood from a turnip. The only monetary recovery we could take solace in was the $1,500 security deposit that we collected when the lease was originally signed.

These difficulties may have been lessened had we done a better job of screening each tenant living in the house. As we mentioned earlier, it is better to leave a property empty for a month than accept a high-risk tenant who could cause twelve months of agony simply because you are desperate. Remember too that every adult living at a property must be screened. Ideally, you will do this process yourself. If you rely on a rental service (as we did) or other people to do the screening, make sure that they do a thorough job.

Never before did we really NEED certain team members so quickly: painters, landscapers, and an aggressive real estate agent to sell the property once certain items were repaired. While the house sat empty and disheveled, we could not collect rent or show it to prospective buyers. We were anxious to get the repairs done. Because of our previously established relationships, the landscapers started immediately instead of putting us at the bottom of their work list. Knowing which painting company does a good, quick job as opposed to a detailed and lengthy job meant we saved two weeks of dead time getting the property ready.

Right then and there, we became the accidental rehabbers. It was a good thing that we bought this property at a bargain price, otherwise it would have become our own real money pit. However, when all the repairs were finished, the house was even more beautiful than when we first bought it. After two years of difficult ownership with horrendous tenants and pricey repairs, the house was now worth about $379,000. That was $150K in hard-earned equity.

At this forced reevaluation point, we decided to change our original exit strategy and sell the property immediately. Paying an extra ten thousand dollars to ensure that we got the property to begin with was ultimately well worth it. We were able to sell the property after two and a half years of ownership for an excellent profit, rather than waiting five years per our original exit strategy.

The profit on Hilltop Garden Drive was large, but the blood, sweat, and tears were large as well. In the end, our team's hard work paid off. So remember, you may buy a property with a very specific exit strategy in mind, but tenants sometimes have a way of forcing an alternate plan. Be flexible and adaptable. Bad things will happen. Expect and plan for them so that you will know what to do if and when things go wrong.

Roundup at Pony Horse

Early in our career we attempted to follow the techniques of a particular real estate guru. To start off, we purchased a lovely new home on Pony Horse Road. Having read a book on rent-to-own and lease options, we intended to recreate the author's wealth using his method. Pony Horse was to be offered as a rent-to-own home. Tenants would lock in a future sales price on the home with a sizable non-refundable deposit, pay monthly rent, and care for the home as if they owned it. We did plenty of advertising for Pony Horse as a rent-to-own, including bandit signs, classified ads, and flyers.

After much effort to promote this idea, but little research into its applicability in our particular market, we learned that the rent-to-own strategy was not the most effective way to fill our houses. In fact, we learned the hard way that this method actually created many legal pitfalls in our area. Most renters in our market did not need to rent-to-own, since home prices were so affordable and interest rates were historically very low. Also, people who could not qualify to purchase a home for one reason or another had very little cash on hand for the required deposit. It took us some time and disappointment before we realized that this approach really did not fit our situation. So, after a quick reevaluation, we decided to offer the home as a regular rental and quickly found a qualified tenant.

Ironically, these tenants did express interest in renting to own this particular home, but stated they would need a few months to accumulate enough money for the deposit. Meanwhile, renting the property, they agreed to care for the home as if it were their own.

Of course, the only time in our entire landlording career that we received the dreaded backed-up toilet call in the middle of the night was from these tenants—the ones who agreed to take care of the house as if it were their own! However, it was we who spent the time working with the builder's warranty company in order to get the plumbing fixed. It was also we who made sure that the sprinklers were working when the trees in the front yard died. Actually, throughout their one-year lease, when any problem arose with the house, it was we who ended up taking care of it. So much for the tenant treating the house as if it were their own!

We later found out that this *was* the way they cared for their own property. When the tenants moved out, they left the house filthy and in desperate need of a new coat of paint. Despite things like footprints on the ceiling, dirty walls everywhere, stained carpets, a torn screen door, and a garage filled with urine and feces from an unauthorized dog, they claimed to have cleaned the house before leaving. Yuck!

You may think that it would have been better had they agreed to purchase the house and take it off our hands. However, we learned very early on that despite their income, the rent payment alone was difficult for them to come up with. Had we signed a contract to sell without the deposit, we would have nothing to show for the legally binding sales agreement. This would have tied up the property, thus not allowing us to sell to anyone else at any time.

We also felt we dodged a bullet because during their year of tenancy the neighborhood experienced an unusual increase in appreciation. When we had originally offered to lock in a sales price for them to purchase the house in two years, we thought $250,000 was a fair price. Because of the amazing market conditions, at the end of one year, the house was already worth $350,000! It would have been painful for us had we handed over the house with all of that equity. Instead, we were ecstatic that our exit strategy was not written in stone and that we were able to alter it according to the situation.

Though extreme market conditions cannot be predicted, we still could have saved ourselves some time and trouble. Another person's success with a method is no guarantee. Methods and techniques are important tools for learning and earning but are not applicable in every market as the self-proclaimed gurus would like you to believe. When you have an entire team backing you up, you are not dependent upon a single viewpoint. Your job is to listen to all of the different viewpoints from your team members and decide for yourself which one fits you and your marketplace.

Risks of Hero Worship

During our journey into real estate investing, we have taken our share of investment seminars from self-proclaimed gurus (as well as many legitimate educators). As discussed earlier in this book, much of the gurus' information is outdated. While many speakers will have some useful information to take home, the next story is indicative of the attitude taken by many of these speakers.

During a break at a seminar, we overheard the main speaker prepping the next presenter. The main speaker whispered, "Let me milk them completely before I turn them over to you." Unfortunately, he was not talking about cows. The main speaker, not surprisingly, went on to push his own products for sale before introducing the next speaker.

As witnessed by this example, speakers often know that their material is no longer, if it ever was, worthy, and are just relying on the showmanship of their presentations. Excitement can be contagious, and gurus will count on this in order to sell their materials. Don't get caught up in these quick and easy approaches to wealth. Remember, a healthy amount of skepticism is important when attending real estate investing seminars or workshops. Determine for yourself whether the speaker's wealth is coming solely from his or her book and CD sales or from the sharing of valuable information.

Please keep in mind that every seminar speaker is not exemplified by this story. Robert Kiyosaki's approach, for example, is to act like an educator, not a used car salesman. He encourages his students to learn new ways of gathering and processing information in order to become more successful wealth builders. By doing so, he rightly encourages an individual to find a method that best fits his or her personality and style, instead of simply having students memorize and then regurgitate specific techniques. We strongly endorse this kind of education since it leaves the final decisions and responsibilities in the right hands: yours.

You have to learn how to find the information before you can find your own method of investing. Investing in real estate is most effective when you take a common sense approach with a powerful team of advisors bringing up the rear. There is no magic involved, but if done well, the rewards can be magical!

Tenant MVPs

Most interactions with tenants are not disastrous. In fact, property management can provide its own little rewards. This usually happens with tenants that you screen very thoroughly.

While many tenants will require occasional poking and prodding to get them to pay rent, you will come across tenants who are very responsible. For example, a particular tenant calls us near the end of every month to let us know that he dropped off the rent check at our office. Wow! This may seem like a small thing to most, but it makes our day. To top it off, this same tenant regularly drops off the rent check a week early! We were very pleased with our choice of tenant and his actions reaffirmed that our screening process can work.

Another tenant impressed us despite her occasional trouble getting the rent to us on time. She always paid in full and informed us if she needed an extra day or two. She maintained the house to very high standards. This stay-at-home mom made sure that the house was always tidy and looking like a model home. When it came time to sell the house, no one believed that a family of five lived there. This family had actually been turned down by other landlords because of credit issues. However, our screening process included a personal meeting that allowed us to see the family as a whole, instead of merely as a credit score.

It is these kinds of tenants whom you should reward sometime during their lease with simple gestures like small gift certificates to a local grocery store. In order to encourage tenants like these to lengthen their leases, also consider replacing or upgrading an appliance of their choice, as mentioned earlier, or even painting the walls a neutral color of their choice. Actions like these will help create good feelings between tenant and landlord. These kind actions are usually well received and appreciated. Tenants feel that you are looking out for them instead of simply trying to nickel-and-dime them. Sure, you will get people who will not appreciate these types of gestures, but in general most will.

Another reward for landlording is simply the thanks that tenants will give you for a job well done. When a tenant tells you that they appreciate all that you have done and are thankful for your patience, you will feel really good. Sometimes a thank you can come in the form of not hearing from a tenant except when you receive their rent payments on time. Basically, if nothing bad happens on any given day when you are a landlord, consider that a good day.

Unfortunately in real estate, there will be situations when you feel no kindness or sympathy towards a tenant, a lender, an underwriter, a buyer, or a seller. In these cases, unless you have been severely mistreated or wronged, take the high road and avoid any major conflict if possible. Recalling the simplest thanks and goodwill gestures from good tenants during these moments can help make up for frustrations caused by other tenants.

Chapter 9

Deflecting Naysayers and Doomsayers

Padded with lots of information, a brilliant game plan, and a fantastic team, you are finally ready to get in the game. Be prepared, though, for the occasional attempted tackle by a naysayer or a doomsayer. We've touched on these people briefly and we don't mean to scare you off, but unfortunately, they are part of any investing endeavor. Just like crabs pulling other crabs down, there will be other people who will try their hardest to pull you down in order to keep you from succeeding. Who are these people? Unfortunately, they are often the people we call friends and family.

For whatever reasons, these loved ones find it easier to be spiteful, jealous, or obstructionist than to learn and profit from your experience in real estate. You will need to decide which is more important to you: the approval of certain family members and friends, or financial security for you and your family. You may need to break with tradition or behave in ways that you were taught were only for the "rich." Unfortunately, it can often come to these kinds of decisions.

Don't automatically trust the advice of any one person, even if he or she is a trusted family member or even an expert in their field. You must research any information independently to either verify or disprove it before acting on it.

Family and friends may become confused with your growing expertise in real estate. Oftentimes with human nature, if something is foreign, it may be automatically feared and disliked, even demonized. We experienced this from one friend who couldn't decide whether to berate us or join us. She e-mailed us saying that many real estate "experts" suggested that the "real estate bubble was going to crash" very soon. In this case, she attributed this viewpoint to two well-known stock investors! She then recommended that we listen to them and pull out of real estate before all of our money was lost. However, on the very next day, this same friend e-mailed us asking why we were not including her in any of our upcoming real estate deals! Which is it? Was real estate investing a bad idea to her or did she want in on the profits? We couldn't tell. Essentially, she slapped us in the face with one hand, and then asked us for a handout with the other one. Talk about mixed messages.

Obviously this friend was very conflicted. Because she did not know how to invest in real estate, she chose to rely on external sources (stock investors in this case) for all of her opinions. Her fear and uncertainty led her to block out all of the great information available to her and to ultimately take the easier and safer route of being a doomsayer.

This leads us to the loudest, and probably most influential, group of naysayers and doomsayers: the media. As soon as a person's opinion is printed on paper, the public will view that person as an expert on the subject regardless of the person's integrity. Journalists do have a tough job in that they have a limited period of time to learn about a subject and then create a coherent and accurate report about it. Unfortunately, they are sometimes not even in the ballpark and report misinformation as fact. Regardless of the reason for this erroneous information, they can have a profound effect on our lives. This certainly holds true in the world of real estate investing.

An online news source reporting on the "booming Phoenix real estate market" mentioned in its article that the population growth in Phoenix of nearly 100,000 new residents per year has resulted in an increase in housing starts as well as rising prices. However, in the next paragraph, the author angrily claimed that investors from California and Las Vegas were responsible for "*artificially* driving up prices and demand." Again, which is it? What was causing the increase in demand and prices—a rapidly growing local population or those nasty out-of-state investors? This journalist allowed his own prejudices to cloud the reality of the situation.

Real estate investors are often blamed for any negatively perceived changes that occur in local housing markets. While it is true that investors can influence a market's rise up or its slide down, it is certainly other factors that actually create the rise or fall. In fact, a good investor will see a change in the market before most people and will act accordingly to create wealth. Good investors don't make the boom or bust, but instead successfully ride the wave up and down.

Okay, so who can you trust? And whose advice do you listen to? There is only one person who knows exactly what your goals and needs are: you. No one person has all the answers for any subject pertaining to real estate. The key is to know a little about a lot so that you can pick the right experts for your situation. You have to listen to what many "experts" in a particular field have to say, extract pertinent info, and then form your own ideas and actions.

Real estate markets are always in flux, depending mainly on factors that involve supply and demand. Since people are always moving for one reason or another, the housing market is also on the move, although it does not change nearly as quickly as the stock market. Unfortunately, some authors and many seminar speakers do not alter their courses to fit these changing markets.

Again, this is not to say that there are no worthwhile speakers or authors on the subject of real estate investing. People like Kiyosaki are out there encouraging people to begin what is a lifelong process of learning—at least, lifelong if you want to truly be successful at it. David Lereah, the chief economist for the National Association of Realtors® (NAR), is also trying to educate people regarding the housing market. His book *Why the Real Estate Boom Will Not Bust—And How You Can Profit from It* successfully reveals what factors are important when considering investing in real estate or even when buying your own home. Books and other resources are out there. It is simply a matter of wading through the information to find what is relevant for your goals.

Please don't let this chapter discourage you. Embrace those friends and family that do support you or join you. Reward them with assistance in becoming involved with real estate investing. On a more positive note, if your spouse or significant other is just as interested in getting involved with real estate as you are, then the learning and earning process will be much easier and more efficient, not to mention more enjoyable, together. You cannot expect the same amount of enthusiasm from everybody, but when you find it that mutual understanding is priceless.

As for those people who prefer to act more like crabs than humans, simply ignore them. Insulate yourself from this kind of person with your knowledge and your respected team members. Don't let doomsayers and naysayers derail you from your important track to success. Do not let them undo your hard work. For this reason, pick your investing partners very carefully.

Chapter 10

House of Knowledge

Constant Reevaluation

The mind of a successful real estate investor is constantly burning through new ideas and methods related to investing. Doing this regularly is a great exercise for your brain. When you have an idea that you believe may be useful, bounce it off one of your team members and evaluate it thoroughly. By reevaluating yourself and your ideas constructively, it allows you to take a chance on an investment that, if measured twice and cut once—so to speak—may prove to be very profitable and successful.

Use and Reward Your Team

Now that you have assembled an all-star team, utilize its members' strengths. Then, please remember to reward those team members who have been kind, loyal, and constantly helpful to you.

Like the title of a 2000 Warner Brothers movie says, remember to *pay it forward*. Let team members know that they are vital to your success in real estate. As part of a team, they will feel valued. Just as we recommend you do with tenants, reward your advisors. A greeting card or a small gift at holidays (or better yet, at random times) can create good will and remind them of your existence. (And remember, business gifts of up to $25 are tax deductible. So keep the receipts.) Make each valued member feel as important as they truly are.

As your experience expands, you will need to reevaluate individual team members often. If there is a concern with a particular advisor, review his or her performance and decide for yourself whether he or she is still the best person for the job. People and situations change; some for better, some for worse. Oftentimes, an individual teammate can become too content and even lazy because they believe that they have your complete loyalty no matter what they do. If an advisor has been very effective in the past, but no longer fills your needs, start the search again immediately. Make a change before a major problem occurs.

Learn and Earn

Be open to learning new information. Continue reading books on investing in real estate and general economics. Read or skim through books on familiar topics. You will likely pick up a few new ideas.

Occasionally you should even read books and articles written by people who have negative and opposing viewpoints on real estate investing, i.e. written by naysayers and doomsayers. If you ultimately find that a naysayer's theory is flawed, then you will have further affirmed your own viewpoint. Don't only read books, articles, and magazines that support your investing methods and theories. Learn at least some information about negative and opposing viewpoints. Without doing so you are not fully assessing the likely success of your methods and you are not limiting your risk and exposure to unwanted outcomes as much you possibly can. Thorough research can go a long way to supporting ultimate success.

Even in housing markets that are cruising along solidly with good economics to back them up, you will find books touting imminent bursting bubbles and claiming that economic doom is inevitable. Let's say that you come across a book claiming that a housing market bubble is about to burst and that many people will lose huge amounts of money as a result. This should be of at least some concern to you since you have created a small real estate empire. Then, suddenly, the book becomes a *New York Times* bestseller and stirs fear into you and the general population. Discussions at cocktail parties turn from making money in real estate to avoiding losing everything. An inexperienced investor may look at the front and back covers, then run to his or her agent to begin selling every property before the so-called bubble bursts. Before buying into an author's predictions, we urge you to get a copy of the book and read it, or at least skim it, to see if it deserves any merit.

Then, after conducting more research on the Internet, with newspapers, and other sources, you can verify or disprove the author's theories. If the author makes some salient points that fit current market and economic conditions, then you can delve further into particular issues. If the ideas are reasonably verifiable elsewhere, then you can take the appropriate action necessary to avoid major problems.

On the other hand, if you decide that the author's arguments are based upon weak assumptions which are counter to all of the research and knowledge that you have accumulated, then you can allay most, if not all, of your fears. Now you can comfortably move on to other projects. In this way, you become an informed and active participant in your future instead of blindly listening and reacting to naysayers and doomsayers who do not have your best interests at heart.

Your task is to differentiate between fact, fiction, and prediction. No matter what their credentials are, authors and experts put a spin on whatever they are saying. Your job is to decipher what they are saying based upon your own knowledge. Always consider the source. It's not easy, but also look at graphs, charts, and photos presented by an author with a careful eye. Ask yourself, do these images jive with their spin? Do they meld with your knowledge? Who are their sources and are they reliable?

It is important to question bold statements until you can verify or disprove them independently. Have some healthy skepticism until you have rationally convinced yourself that something is true. After all, your financial security is dependent upon it. Sure, it would be great if every stock tip that Uncle Harry gave you was a good one, but since he spends most of his time at a nine-to-five job that's unrelated to investing, he probably really hasn't a clue. Do not blindly trust any one person for all of your answers. Their information may fit their needs and goals, but it may not work for yours. Collect data, make sense of it, test it, and then apply it accordingly. This way, you will reasonably limit any information or processes that do not fit your goals.

Read voraciously. New books, articles, studies, and papers become available every day. Information is the building block that creates knowledge. And from that knowledge, you can construct action appropriate to your situation.

With the Internet, you can read an article one minute and go to another site the next minute to either verify or disprove the first article's theories. This is a relatively new luxury for the small investor. It is probably another reason why so many people are now involved in real estate investing.

Resources

The Internet can be a great tool for investing. Following is a list of some helpful sites that can provide you with hours and hours of free research.

www.realtor.com and www.realtor.org

Realtor.com is the official website for the National Association of Realtors®. You can access properties for sale throughout the country by simply providing some basic information. Realtor.org also posts tons of economic and housing data that is broken down into national, state, and county numbers. These are extremely useful sites and no membership is required.

www.realtytimes.com

This website provides real estate news from around the country. In its "local market conditions" section, real estate agents provide their opinion on the housing market in their particular locale. It allows you to get a sense of what is going on in that area without actually having to visit.

www.ofheo.gov

This site is sponsored by the Office of Federal Housing Enterprise Oversight. A great site for researching housing prices of both past and present, by major city or state. It has tons and tons of good info that can help you spot trends.

www.census.gov

Going through this site thoroughly would take months. The number of applications for the data is limitless. The major census poll is done every ten years, while smaller updates return every two years. So the data is always relatively fresh and relevant. Don't miss this one.

www.bls.gov and www.bea.gov

These are the official sites for the Bureau of Labor Statistics and the Bureau of Economic Analysis. They provide data on unemployment, jobs, and other economic data by regions. This is a great tool if you are looking for signs of growth in certain areas in order to anticipate the next boomtown or slowdown.

www.hsh.com and www.bankrate.com

These two sites concentrate on all things financial. Their calculators are very useful when running numbers for a potential investment property.

www.homedepot.com, www.lowes.com, and www.walmart.com

If you need repairs, look no further.

www.overstock.com

Okay, this doesn't have much to do with real estate, but it is one of our favorite sites to shop on the web. You would be amazed what items you can find for around the house. If you plan to rent your property as a furnished rental, then this site will be of great assistance.

www.zillow.com

This amazing website compiles home sales information from around the country and comes up with an estimate value for a particular address. Best of all, there is no requirement to divulge any personal information to use its database and it is free!

The website of the economics department at your local university or college

Many times, students and professors will compile useful local economic and housing data and place it all on their department's website. They often use data from federal agencies but will add numbers from local sources that the federal agencies might not have access to. Thus, the information may be even more accurate and up to date than the data from the federal government.

Decisions, Decisions

There is usually more than one way to do something. In order to succeed in real estate (and in life), you have to get comfortable with choices and making final and binding decisions. There is risk involved, but there are many ways to minimize that risk. Since there are different pathways to success, there can be multiple right answers to any one question. However, many people prefer to view the world and all of its complexities as being only black or white. Unfortunately for these people, there actually exists plenty of gray in the world. Sometimes in life there are no answers, just choices.

Stop looking for the perfect answer to your question or problem and start looking at the possibilities that are in front of you.

Don't look for something that does not exist, like the *perfect* lease agreement or the *perfect* loan. Instead, use the rules and foundations that do exist to find the best fit. Add clauses to a contract if something is missing or refinance the loan AFTER you take possession of a property, instead of dragging out escrow. In other words, don't make things more difficult than they have to be. Opt for the simplest path when possible.

If you want to change something that has been done in a certain way for years and years, realize that, yes, you might be able to change it, but ask yourself if it is worth the hassle. If it is, then good luck and go to it. Otherwise, the system in place will still offer ample opportunities for you to create abundant wealth for you and your loved ones while also helping other people.

Take control of your future by taking responsibility for your actions. Advisors may help direct the process, but it all comes down to your decisions. It is essential that you understand and agree with this. It is for this reason that we recommend having a team to help you make these decisions. When it comes to investing in real estate, base your decisions and actions on verifiable information or trustworthy sources, not on emotions.

It is okay to have emotions, though. Actually, it's inescapable. You can like a property, as long as you can also separate yourself from that viewpoint and look at the property as an asset when it comes time to buy or sell it.

The No-Compete Clause

Real estate investing can truly be profitable and enjoyable. You provide a basic need for people while creating supplemental or primary income for you and your family. By this time it is clear that the analogy of real estate investing as a team sport is important, because in this field you will have to rely on others for support, leadership, advice, and guidance.

However, real estate investing should not be a competitive sport—unless you are competing with yourself, of course. There are plenty of money, deals, properties, and opportunities to go around for everybody. So relax and enjoy. Don't lose sight of your goals even though they may change along the way.

Oftentimes during a real estate investing seminar, you will sit next to someone who will immediately ask you, upon seating, "How many properties do you have?" or "How many did you get using so-and-so's techniques?" Ironically, these same people are often the ones who will make a career out of taking these seminars. They rarely practice what is taught and own few, if any, properties. Do not let these goofballs get you down! Remember that real estate investing is to help you, your family, and your friends, not to one-up Uncle Billy, your friend Jim, or the guy sitting next to you in a seminar. Creating wealth is not a competition.

Patience

Patience is absolutely required every step of the way. Patience with yourself, your team members, the market, and most definitely your significant other is mandatory! Once you've made a decision, the world doesn't always just fall into place. Real estate investing can test your resolve. Some fights are worth the effort, but other conflicts that don't affect your end goal should be avoided. Remember to keep looking at the big picture at first, then, as you become more comfortable with things, concentrate on the details one at a time but in the order of their importance. Prioritize!

And Finally...

Please remember to reward those who help you along the way. Charity really does start at *home*! If you wait until you are rich in order to reward someone with a gift or a bonus then you are missing the point of having this money. Share some of your wins with your team members during the game, not just afterward. Your team of advisors and support team will appreciate this more than you realize. Also, every year, give money to charities in at least small amounts. Again, don't wait until you can present that one big fat check to a charity. Finally, remember that both gifts to business associates and charities are tax-deductible in the year that they are given.

So read up, listen up, watch, and learn. Then, when you are ready, get out there and start wisely investing in real estate. As a character in the movie *Star Wars: The Empire Strikes Back* once said, "Do or do not. There is no Try."

We are confident that when all is said and done, investing in real estate will enrich your life. Hopefully, much of what we have shared with you in this book will help you along your journey to boundless wealth in real estate. We wish you the best.

Glossary

AMORTIZATION
The reduction of a debt or mortgage by making regular payments towards the principal of a loan.

APPRAISER
A person trained and licensed to determine the value of a certain property using different methods.

APPRECIATION
An increase in the value of a property above and beyond the original purchase price.

APPRECIATION RATE
Expressed as a percentage, this rate is the amount of appreciation divided by the original purchase price. Thus, the higher the appreciation, the higher the appreciation rate.

ADJUSTABLE RATE MORTGAGE or ARM
A type of loan that has a fixed interest rate for a given time, after

which time the interest rate becomes variable, based on a certain financial index. Examples include 1/1, 3/1, 5/1, 7/1, or 10/1 ARMs. The first number denotes the time period, in years, that the interest rate is fixed. The second number signifies how often, in years, that the interest rate will be adjusted after the initial fixed period.

CAPITAL GAIN
The amount of profit made from the sale of a property.

CASH FLOW
The amount of money (or deficit, if negative) that remains after all property expenses are paid and accounted for.

CASH FLOW, AFTER TAX
This is the amount of profit or loss that remains after one's personal or corporate tax liability is taken into account. For most small investors, the after-tax cash flow will be higher than the before-tax cash flow. This is a very important concept to understanding today's advantages of owning real estate investments.

CHATTELS
A tangible part of a structure or building that is generally removable or easily replaceable. Examples include kitchen appliances, washers and dryers, window coverings, and carpeting.

CONFORMING LOANS
A mortgage loan that is eligible to be bought by Fannie Mae or Freddie Mac on the secondary market.

CONTINGENCY CLAUSE
A clause deftly placed by a real estate agent in a purchaser's or seller's contract stipulating that a certain action must occur before the contract becomes legally binding.

CONVENTIONAL LOANS

A mortgage loan that is guaranteed by an entity *other* than the Federal Housing Authority or the Veterans Administration. Commonly used to describe a mortgage loan that has a fixed rate and a fixed term.

CRABS

Slang for those people who, because of their own lack of success and their personal discontent, attempt to keep others from succeeding.

DEPRECIATION

Specified by the federal government, this amount represents, in dollars, how much a building has decreased in value over a period of time. The amount can be used to legally decrease one's tax liability. Residential property is depreciated over 27.5 years or 3.63 percent per year, while commercial property is generally depreciated over 39 years or 2.56 percent per year. Example: an investor buys a single-family home for $100,000 which has a building value of $75,000 and a land value of $25,000 as determined by the local governing body. Therefore, each year, the investor may take a $2,727 tax deduction due to the building's depreciation. The land is not considered depreciable; therefore, its value is not included when computing depreciation amounts.

DOOMSAYERS

People who have a very pessimistic view of life. They are usually very unhappy and unsuccessful people. See also *Naysayers*.

EQUITY BUILDUP

As a mortgage is amortized over the term of the loan, the original principal amount of the loan decreases, thus creating equity even if the value of the property remains the same. This only applies to mortgages that include monthly principal payments.

ESCROW

The process that must occur when a buyer and seller enter into a sales contract. In order to avoid any conflict of interests, this process is carried out by a neutral entity such as an escrow and title company or a lawyer.

FORECLOSURE

This occurs when an owner defaults on his or her loan agreement (usually by not paying the monthly mortgage), and the lender begins the legal process that will terminate the owner's rights to the property and any equity associated with it.

FANNIE MAE or FNMA

A pseudonym for the Federal National Mortgage Association, a semi-private corporation that buys mortgages from mortgage bankers on the secondary market. They are regulated by The Office of Federal Housing Enterprise and Oversight (OFHEO), a federal agency.

FEDERAL HOUSING ADMINISTRATION or FHA

A division of the U.S. Department of Housing and Urban Development (HUD). They administer and guarantee many types of loans, especially for those who do not have enough money for a typical down payment.

FSBO

For Sale By Owner. This occurs when a property owner attempts to sell his or her property without the help of a licensed real estate agent. Pronounced "fizbo."

HAZARD INSURANCE

A policy that, when purchased appropriately, protects the legal owner of a property from paying all of the costs of damage due to such things as fires, storms, and other natural disasters.

HUD
The U.S. Department of Housing and Urban Development creates, implements, and enforces certain minimum housing standards for all citizens.

INTEREST-ONLY LOAN
A particular loan with payments to a lender that only covers interest. This results in no net decrease in the loan principal, i.e. there is no equity buildup.

LEVERAGE
The ability to borrow money from another person, bank, or other entity in order to purchase a property using little or no money of your own. Leverage greatly increases your purchasing power and ultimately the profitability of a property.

LIMITED LIABILITY COMPANY or LLC
A legal corporation allowed by the federal government that can limit the partners' personal financial liability. Also advantageous is that any gains or losses can "flow through" to the partners or managing members' personal taxes. In recent years, LLCs have been a very popular entity from which to hold and manage rental property.

LOAN OFFICER
The person who is in charge of your loan file while it is being approved or denied by the lender. He or she works under the supervision of a mortgage broker.

LOAN REPAYMENT
The reduction of a debt or mortgage by making regular payments toward the principal of a loan. See also *Amortization*.

MORTGAGE
The loan that you repay (to a lender) for money borrowed in order to purchase property. The property is used as collateral by the lender. Originally, a word of Latin and French descent meaning "an agreement [gage] until death [mortir]."

MORTGAGE BROKER
For a fee, this person will shop different investors and lenders in order to find a suitable and competitive loan for you. They will not service the loan once it is in place.

NATIONAL ASSOCIATION OF REALTORS® (NAR)
The National Association of Realtors® is an organization of over 600,000 national Realtors® who, among other things, are required to abide by the CODE OF ETHICS set forth by the NAR. See www.realtor.com and www.realtor.org for more information.

NAYSAYERS
People who are constantly attempting to discourage others by saying something cannot be done. They are usually unsuccessful and unhappy people. See also *Doomsayers*.

NOTE
A written agreement of a debt and a promise to pay it back. For example, a *mortgage* is a note that uses the home as collateral should the owner default on his or her payments.

PRINCIPAL
The amount owed on a loan, not including interest. Usually, the original amount borrowed.

QUALIFIED INTERMEDIARY
A person or entity that has the appropriate legal credentials to handle a 1031 exchange transaction. Also called an *accommodator*.

REAL ESTATE LICENSEE

This is a person who has passed certain state and federal require-ments in order to represent buyers and sellers in a real estate transaction. A real estate licensee is required to "hang" their license with a real estate broker. In order to become a Realtor®, a licensee must also take and pass a test administered by the NAR and its state divisions. Also called *agents.*

REAL ESTATE BROKER

A licensed real estate agent who, with certain required experience, has chosen to take additional classes and training required by his or her state in order to become a broker. A broker is allowed to have other agents "hang" their licenses with their brokerage in return for an agreed-upon fee. He or she provides guidance and services to licensees and are ultimately responsible for the agents' actions. The broker may or may not be a Realtor®.

RECAPTURE TAX

When an investment property is sold for a gain, the federal govern-ment levies this tax against the depreciation that was taken for your own tax reduction during your span of ownership. It is taxed at a 25 percent rate and will be recaptured whether or not you actually took the deductions each year. Therefore, it is wise to hire a professional to ensure that these deductions are properly taken every year.

SECONDARY MORTGAGE MARKET

A system that allows corporations such as Fannie Mae or Freddie Mac to buy residential mortgages from small and large mortgage bankers and lenders. By doing so, the system frees up money in local markets for the continuation of financing more properties.

SPOUSE or SIGNIFICANT OTHER

The one person in your life that you can always count on.

TAX DEDUCTION

Particular and specified spending that reduces taxable income. The actual amount of tax reduction will depend on that company's or that person's final tax rate.

TAX CREDIT

A dollar-for-dollar reduction in tax liability regardless of a person's ultimate tax rate.

TENANCY-IN-COMMON or TIC

An arrangement of real ownership between two and thirty-five parties in which each party has an undivided interest in the property. TIC syndicates are created in order to bring small investors together on larger properties that individually would be too expensive for the small investor. In many of these syndicates, the day-to-day management and accounting is done by the syndicate and profits are distributed to investors on a monthly basis. This is a hands-off approach to real estate investing but, if done correctly, can allow the small investor to reap the profits of larger properties with mitigated risks.

1031 EXCHANGE

The section of the Internal Revenue Code that allows an investor to use proceeds from a sale in order to purchase another investment property, without incurring any tax on the capital gains. There are very specific rules tied to this type of exchange, but when used properly a 1031 exchange can defer one's tax liability indefinitely.

TITLE

Proof of ownership in a written form that is recorded at your local recorder's office.

TITLE COMPANY

An entity that researches title to real property and oftentimes offers title insurance. In many cases the escrow and title companies are one and the same.

TITLE INSURANCE
An insurance policy that protects the policy holder against any abnormalities in title.

UMBRELLA POLICY
An insurance policy that takes effect after all other appropriate insurance policies have reached their maximum coverage.

UNDERWRITER
The person responsible for approving or denying a particular loan application for a given investor. The underwriter works for the lender and minimizes taking on risky loans. Unfortunately for the investor, underwriters can often be naysayers due to the often rigid formulas that they employ.

Appendix B

References and Recommended Reading

* * *

Bernstein, Peter W., ed., *The Ernst and Young Tax Guide 2006.* New York: CDS Books, 2005.

Campbell, Robert M. *Timing the Real Estate Market.* California: The Campbell Method, 2002.

Cummings, Jack. *The Tax-Free Exchange Loophole: How Real Estate Investors Can Profit from the 1031 Exchange.* New Jersey: John Wiley & Sons, 2005.

de Roos, PhD, Dolf. *Real Estate Riches: How to Become Rich Using Your Banker's Money.* New Jersey: John Wiley & Sons, 2005.

Guttentag, Jack. *The Mortgage Encyclopedia: An Authoritative Guide to Mortgage Programs, Practices, Prices, and Pitfalls.* Wisconsin: CWL Publishing Enterprises, Inc., 2004.

Harris, Jack C., and Jack P. Friedman. *Barron's Real Estate Hand-book*. New York: Baron's Educational Services, Inc., 2001.

Hendricks, Evan. *Credit Scores & Credit Reports: How the System Really Works, What You Can Do.*, Maryland: Privacy Times, Inc., 2005.

Hoven, Vernon. *The Real Estate Investor's Tax Guide: What Every Investor Needs to Know to Maximize Profits*. Illinois: Dearborn Real Estate Education, 2005.

Irwin, Robert. *The Landlord's Troubleshooter*. Illinois: Dearborn Financial Publishing Inc., 1999.

Kennedy, CPA, Diane. *Loopholes of the Rich: How The Rich Legally Make More Money & Pay Less Tax*. New York: Warner Books, 2001.

Kiyosaki, Robert T., and Sharon L. Lechter. *Rich Dad, Poor Dad: What the Rich Teach Their Kids About Money—That the Poor and Middle Class Do Not!* New York: Warner Business Books, 2000.

Kiyosaki, Robert T., and Sharon Lechter. *Cashflow Quadrant: Rich Dad's Guide to Financial Freedom*. New York: Warner Business Books, 2000.

Lereah, David. *Why the Real Estate Boom Will Not Bust—And How You Can Profit from It: How to Build Wealth in Today's Expanding Real Estate Market*. New York: Random House, Inc., 2005.

Mancuso, Anthony. *Your Limited Liability Company: An Operating Manual*. California: Nolo, 2002.

McElroy, Ken. *The ABCs of Real Estate Investing: The Secrets of Finding Hidden Profits Most Investors Miss*. New York: Warner Business Books, 2004.

McKenzie, Dennis J. and Richard M. Betts. *Essentials of Real Estate Economics.* Ohio: Thomson South-Western, 2006.

Ross, George H. *Trump Strategies for Real Estate: Billionaire Lessons for the Small Investor.* New Jersey: John Wiley & Sons, Inc., 2005.

Schumacher, Ph.D., David. *Buy and Hold: 7 Steps to a Real Estate Fortune.* New York: Schumacher Enterprises, 2000.

Sirota, David. *Essentials of Real Estate Investment.* Illinois: Dearborn Financial Publishing, Inc., 2004.

Socrates Media (ed.), *The Complete Landlording Handbook.* Illinois: Socrates Media, LLC, 2006.

Stone, Martin and Spencer Strauss, *The Unofficial Guide to Real Estate Investing.* New York: IDG Books Worldwide, 1999.

Thomsett, Michael C., and Jean Freestone Thomsett. *Getting Started in Real Estate.* New Jersey: John Wiley & Sons, 1998.

Trass, Kieran. *Grow Rich with the Property Cycle.* New York: Penguin Books, 2004.

Index

About the Authors

Sheri Alford, Realtor® comes to real estate from a varied background with jobs in nearly a half-dozen industries. Combining organizational and people skills honed as an actress, optician, and event planner, she has finally found her niche in residential real estate. Sheri appreciates the potential to provide quality housing while still making an honest profit. Financial freedom was never something she expected from life; however, Sheri is enormously grateful for what real estate provides her. She loves that she can make her own hours doing something she loves with her husband and partner.

Ahmet Ucmakli, M.D. worked most of his life to become a family physician. Unfortunately, once he achieved this goal, he found that the healthcare community was not truly focused on caring for others. Instead, it was now a business that put doctors on a rigorous factory-like schedule and the bottom line ahead of patients' needs. Instead of succumbing to a lifetime of this grind, Ahmet looked to a powerful financial lesson from his parents involving the houses he grew up in. While his parents lost significant amounts of money in the stock market, they always managed to create wealth whenever they sold their own house, even amidst the worst housing-market downturns!

Inspired by this success, Sheri and Ahmet spent lots of time and money educating themselves, discovering how to profitably buy, manage, and sell residential properties. Having amassed their own real estate portfolio worth many millions of dollars, they have also happily worked with a handful of other investors to create tremendous profits. Through their published works and many public appearances, Ahmet and Sheri reveal timeless investing principles so that others may achieve their own financial and personal freedom.

✳ ✳ ✳

www.tamtampress.com